BUILD YOUR ENGLISH SKILLS WITH RUSKIN BOND

Celebrating
30 Years of Publishing
in India

Build your English Skills with Ruskin Bond

ILLUSTRATIONS
Neeta Gangopadhyay

HarperCollins*Children'sBooks*

First published in India in 2022 by HarperCollins Children's Books
An imprint of HarperCollins *Publishers*
Building No. 10, Tower A, 4th Floor, DLF Cyber City,
Phase II, Gurugram, 122002, India
www.harpercollins.co.in

2 4 6 8 10 9 7 5 3 1

P-ISBN: 9789356295445
E-ISBN: 9789356295452

The excerpts included in the book are the original texts from a range of classics (all in the public domain). They have not been edited for spelling or grammar, so as to give the reader a flavour of the original writing.

Typeset in Minion Pro 12 pt/17 pt
by Veena, Bookwatch

Printed and bound at Nutech Print Services - India

CONTENTS

INTRODUCTION

This very special book has been put together with the primary aim of helping students to appreciate the English language and to acquire fluency in it. At the same time, we hope its content will help to inculcate in the reader a love for reading, for literature, and for good writing.

The editorial team at HarperCollins Children's has taken great care in helping me to make this selection of poems and extracts from English children's classics. Notes, questions and suggestions have been provided to help the student, for language changes over the years, and some words and expressions need to be explained.

Some of my own reading favourites appear here – the poems by Walter de la Mare and R.L. Stevenson, the nonsense verse of Edward Lear, the chapters from *Alice in Wonderland, Treasure Island, David Copperfield* and *Three Men in a Boat* among several others.

The chapter from *David Copperfield* takes me back to my school days when, at the age of 12, I read Copperfield and fell in love with the wonderful characters created by Charles Dickens. As a result, I wanted to be a writer too. And eventually I became one.

Books can influence us in many ways. They bring us knowledge, entertainment, a thirst for travel and adventure, and an understanding of human nature. Above all, they help us to think. Unlike other forms of entertainment, reading a book requires some mental effort and participation on the part of the reader.

I would like every student to acquire a strong command of the English language. Fluency in writing and speaking English will give you a tremendous advantage as you go into the world to make a living and carve out a career for yourself. Great literature gives you a sound foundation.

In the course of the last hundred years the English language has taken root in many parts of the world, including India. It has become a global language —the language of science, of commerce, of diplomacy, of international communication. It has absorbed much from other languages and is constantly evolving.

Thousands of young Indians have made their mark abroad—in education, in politics, in technology, in business—and their achievements have come about largely through their command of the English language.

At home in India, parents by the hundreds of thousands are eager to see their children learn English in addition to Hindi and their mother tongue.

Mastery over a language comes from a solid foundation. You must use it, speak it, write it. Above all, you must read in it.

Join us on this exciting literary journey. It will take you forward in more ways than one.

Ruskin Bond

RUSKIN BOND

1
Who Has Seen the Wind?

Who has seen the wind?
Neither I nor you:
But when the leaves hang trembling,
The wind is passing through.

Who has seen the wind?
Neither you nor I:
But when the trees bow down their heads,
The wind is passing by.

Christina Rossetti (1830–1894) was an English writer, who wrote many poems for children on different topics.

FOR DISCUSSION

1. This is a very short poem, but do you think it describes the wind well? What makes it an effective poem?

LANGUAGE

1. This poem has a lot of repetition—many repeated words and phrases. They give it a nice rhythmic feel. Can you identify them?
2. The poet uses a simple inversion of words to change the rhyme between the two stanzas. The second line of the first stanza ends '... I nor you' to rhyme with the fourth line ending of '... passing through'.
   The second line of the second stanza ends '... you nor I' to rhyme with '... passing by'.

   Can you think of another way to say 'neither you or I/neither I or you'? (HINT: Use other pronouns or conjunctions.)
3. This poem uses strong visual imagery to talk about something that cannot be seen. Visual imagery is when words are used to create an image or a picture in our heads about the thing being described.

   Can you think of another visual image that can be used to describe the wind blowing?
4. Using the ideas, words and images that you have thought of in the previous questions, can you add another stanza to the poem?

2
Tom Becomes a Water-Baby

Tom, when he woke, for of course he woke—children always wake after they have slept exactly as long as is good for them—found himself swimming about in the stream, being about four inches, or—that I may be accurate—3.87902 inches long, and having round the **parotid** region of his **fauces** a set of external gills (I hope you understand all the big words) just like those of a sucking **eft**, which he mistook for a lace frill, till he pulled at them, found he hurt himself, and made up his mind that they were part of himself, and best left alone.

In fact, the fairies had turned him into a water-baby.

A water-baby? You never heard of a water-baby. Perhaps not. That is the very reason why this story was written. There are a great many things in the world

Charles Kingsley (1819–1875) was a priest, poet, novelist and historian. This excerpt is from *The Water-Babies, A Fairy Tale for a Land Baby.*

One day, Tom is accused of stealing from a rich man's house, and he runs away to escape from the people chasing him. He jumps into a river which takes him deep into a forest. There, as he sleeps peacefully, something magical happens and Tom turns into a water-baby. In this passage, the author tries to prove that water-babies are as real as fairies. Read the passage to find out what his arguments are.

which you never heard of; and a great many more which nobody ever heard of; and a great many things, too, which nobody will ever hear of.

'But there are no such things as water-babies.' How do you know that? Have you been there to see? And if you had been there to see, and had seen none, that would not prove that there were none. If you do not find a fox in the woods that does not prove that there are no such things as foxes. And no one has a right to say that no water-babies exist, till they have seen no water-babies existing; which is quite a different thing, mind, from not seeing water-babies; and a thing which nobody ever did or perhaps ever will do.

'But surely if there were water-babies, somebody would have caught one at least?'

Well. How do you know that somebody has not?

'But they would have put it into spirits, or into the *Illustrated News*, or perhaps cut it into two halves poor dear little thing, and sent one to Professor Owen and one to Professor Huxley, to see what they would each say about it.'

Ah, my dear little man! That does not follow at all.

'But a water-baby is contrary to nature.'

Well, but, you must learn to talk about such things, when you grow older, in a very different way from that. You must not talk about different way from that. You must not talk about 'ain't' and 'can't' when you speak of this great wonderful world round you, of which the wisest man knows only the very smallest comer, and is, as the great Sir Isaac Newton said, only a child picking up pebbles on the shore of a boundless ocean.

You must not say that this cannot be, or that that is contrary to nature. You do not know what Nature is, or what she can do; and nobody knows.

[There] are dozens and hundreds of things in the world which we should certainly have said were contrary to nature, if we did not see them going on under our eyes all day long. If people had never seen little seeds grow into great plants and trees, of quite different shape from themselves, and these trees again produce fresh seeds, to grow into fresh trees, they would have said, 'The thing cannot be; it is contrary to nature.' And they would have been quite as right in saying so, as in saying that most other things cannot be.

Did not learned men, too, hold, till within the last twenty-five years, that a flying dragon was an impossible monster? And do we not now know that there are hundreds of them found fossil up and down the world?* People call them Pterodactyls: but that is only because they are ashamed to call them flying dragons, after denying so long that flying dragons could exist.

Wise men know that their business is to examine what is, and not to settle what is not. They know that there are elephants; they know that there have been flying dragons; and the wiser they are, the less inclined they will be to say positively that there are no water-babies.

No water-babies, indeed? Why, wise men of old said that everything on earth had its copy in the water; and you may see that that is, if not quite true, still quite as true as most other theories which you are likely to hear for many a day. There are land-babies—then why not water-babies?

Do not even you know that a green **drake**, and an **alderfly**, and a dragonfly, live under water till they change their skins, just as Tom changed his? And if

* as used in the original

a water animal can continually change into a land animal, why should not a land animal sometimes change into a water animal?

Am I in earnest? Oh dear no! Don't you know that this is a fairy tale, and all fun and pretense; and that you are not to believe one word of it, even if it is true? But at all events, so it happened to Tom. Now if you don't like my story, then go to the schoolroom and learn your multiplication-table, and see if you like that better. Some people, no doubt, would do so. So much the better for us, if not for them. It takes all sorts, they say, to make a world.

WORDS TO KNOW

parotid: salivary gland

fauces: opening at the back of the mouth

eft: developmental stage of a newt, an amphibian

drake: male wild duck

alderfly: water insect

Am I in earnest?: Am I serious?

FOR DISCUSSION

1. In the passage you have read, the author tries to convince the reader that the story he is telling is true. After reading the arguments presented, are you convinced? Why or why not?

2. Why do you think the author is trying so hard to convince the reader? Is he even really trying to convince the reader or is it for fun?

3. The final paragraph is different from the rest of the chapter. Why do you think the author changes his tone?

LANGUAGE

Multiple meanings

Some words have more than one meaning. What do you think is the best meaning of the following words and phrases from the text? Read the text and use a dictionary to confirm the correct meaning.

1. **contrary to:** walking with / against the rules of / looking the same as

2. **to settle:** to decide / to argue / to speak

3. **in earnest:** in a funny way / in a serious way / in an angry way

4. **hold:** keep in hand / think and believe strongly / keep in a particular position

Idiomatic expressions

The author ends with the idiomatic expression, 'it takes all kinds to make the world', meaning to say that there are a lot of different types of people in the world, and that everyone does not need to agree with everyone else.

Here are a few other common expressions with 'world'. Do you know what they mean?

1. Love makes the world go round.
2. The world's your oyster.
3. All the world's a stage.
4. The world is watching.

Chapter structure

Most of this chapter is written as if the author is having a discussion or an argument with his readers. It is structured like a debate.

Can you think of some questions you would have liked to ask the author in this debate?

READING IDEAS

If you liked this story, you could read:

1. FIVE CHILDREN AND IT by Edith Nesbit
2. THE CHILDREN OF THE NEW FOREST by Frederick Marryat

3
A Caucus Race

They were indeed a queer-looking party that assembled on the bank—the birds with draggled feathers, the animals with their fur clinging close to them, and all dripping wet, cross and uncomfortable.

The first question of course was, how to get dry again: they had a consultation about this, and after a few minutes it seemed quite natural to Alice to find herself talking familiarly with them, as if she had known them all her life. Indeed, she had quite a long argument with the Lory, who at last turned sulky, and would only say, 'I am older than you, and must know better'; and this Alice would not allow without knowing how old it was, and, as the Lory positively refused to tell its age, there was no more to be said.

At last the Mouse, who seemed to be a person of authority among them, called

LEWIS CARROLL (1832–1898) wrote stories and poems for children. His most famous book is *Alice's Adventures in Wonderland* from which this extract has been taken.

Alice, a young girl, chases a rabbit in her garden and drops down the rabbit hole. Alice finds herself in a strange and wonderful place that is populated by talking birds and animals. Almost as soon as she reaches this 'wonderland' she finds herself swimming in a large pool with groups of animals and birds. Eventually everyone manages to get out of the water.

out, 'Sit down, all of you, and listen to me! *I'll* soon make you dry enough!' They all sat down at once, in a large ring, with the Mouse in the middle. Alice kept her eyes anxiously fixed on it, for she felt sure she would catch a bad cold if she did not get dry very soon.

'Ahem!' said the Mouse with an important air, 'are you all ready? This is the driest thing I know. Silence all round, if you please! "William the Conqueror, whose cause was favoured by the pope, was soon submitted to by the English, who wanted leaders, and had been of late much accustomed to usurpation and conquest. Edwin and Morcar, the earls of Mercia and Northumbria—"'

'Ugh!' said the Lory, with a shiver.

'I beg your pardon!' said the Mouse, frowning, but very politely: 'Did you speak?'

'Not I!' said the Lory hastily.

'I thought you did,' said the Mouse. '—I proceed. "Edwin and Morcar, the earls of Mercia and Northumbria, declared for him: and even Stigand, the patriotic archbishop of Canterbury, found it advisable—"'

'Found *what*?' said the Duck.

'Found *it*,' the Mouse replied rather crossly: 'of course you know what "it" means.'

'I know what "it" means well enough, when I find a thing,' said the Duck: 'it's generally a frog or a worm. The question is, what did the archbishop find?'

The Mouse did not notice this question, but hurriedly went on, '"—found it advisable to go with Edgar Atheling to meet William and offer him the crown. William's conduct at first was moderate. But the insolence of his Normans—" How are you getting on now, my dear?' it continued, turning to Alice as it spoke.

'As wet as ever,' said Alice in a melancholy tone: 'it doesn't seem to dry me at all.'

'In that case,' said the Dodo solemnly, rising to its feet, 'I move that the meeting adjourn, for the immediate adoption of more **energetic remedies**—'

'Speak English!' said the Eaglet. 'I don't know the meaning of half those long words, and, what's more, I don't believe you do either!' And the Eaglet bent down its head to hide a smile: some of the other birds tittered audibly.

'What I was going to say,' said the Dodo in an offended tone, 'was, that the best thing to get us dry would be a Caucus-race.'

'What *is* a Caucus-race?' said Alice; not that she wanted much to know, but the Dodo had paused as if it thought that *somebody* ought to speak, and no one else seemed inclined to say anything.

'Why,' said the Dodo, 'the best way to explain it is to do it.' (And, as you might like to try the thing yourself, some winter day, I will tell you how the Dodo managed it.)

First it marked out a race-course, in a sort of circle, ('the exact shape doesn't matter,' it said) and then all the party were placed along the course, here and there. There was no 'One, two, three, and away,' but they began running when they liked, and left off when they liked, so that it was not easy to know when the race was over. However, when they had been running half an hour or so, and were quite dry again, the Dodo suddenly called out 'The race is over!' and they all crowded round it, panting, and asking, 'But who has won?'

This question the Dodo could not answer without a great deal of thought, and it sat for a long time with one finger pressed upon its forehead (the position in which you usually see Shakespeare, in the pictures of him), while the rest waited in silence. At last the Dodo said, '*Everybody* has won, and all must have prizes.'

'But who is to give the prizes?' quite a chorus of voices asked.

'Why, *she*, of course,' said the Dodo, pointing to Alice with one finger; and the whole party at once crowded round her, calling out in a confused way, 'Prizes! Prizes!'

Alice had no idea what to do, and in despair she put her hand in her pocket, and pulled out a box of **comfits** (luckily the salt water had not got into it), and handed them round as prizes. There was exactly one apiece all round.

'But she must have a prize herself, you

know,' said the Mouse.

'Of course,' the Dodo replied very gravely. 'What else have you got in your pocket?' he went on, turning to Alice.

'Only a **thimble**,' said Alice sadly.

'Hand it over here,' said the Dodo.

Then they all crowded round her once more, while the Dodo solemnly presented the thimble, saying, 'We beg your acceptance of this elegant thimble'; and, when it had finished this short speech, they all cheered.

Alice thought the whole thing very absurd, but they all looked so grave that she did not dare to laugh; and, as she could not think of anything to say, she simply bowed, and took the thimble, looking as solemn as she could.

WORDS TO KNOW

energetic remedies: active cures
comfit: a small sweet; a sugar-covered seed or nut
thimble: a small metal cap for the thumb used while sewing

FOR DISCUSSION

1. Do you think Alice is really in a magical place?
2. Do you think that listening to something very boring is a good way to get dry?
3. Do the events in the story make any sense at all?
4. Does this story sound as if it is all a dream? Why do you think so?
5. How would you have behaved if you were Alice? Would you have done something different?

LANGUAGE

Can you figure out what these words from the text mean? Choose the correct option.

1. **draggled:** neat and tidy / wet and muddy / stiff and dry
2. **cross:** happy / eager / angry
3. **audibly:** loud enough to be heard / long enough to be bored / too quiet to be understood
4. **solemnly:** in a funny manner / in a serious manner / in a easy manner
5. **grave:** serious / sleepy / happy

Multiple meanings

In this story, many characters misunderstand words. For example, the Mouse says that he is going to dry everyone out by telling them the driest thing he knows. Here, the situation is created by the fact that the word 'dry' has two different meanings: the first is the opposite of 'wet'; the second, which the Mouse understands it as, is 'boring' or 'uninteresting'. That is why the Mouse thinks it is a good idea to tell them the most boring thing he knows.

1. The term 'caucus race' is not really a race. Find out what it is.
2. The Dodo uses very complicated language which the Eaglet cannot understand. Use a dictionary to figure out what the Dodo was trying to say. (If you wish, try that for what the Mouse says.)

READING IDEAS

If you liked this story, you could read:

1. THROUGH THE LOOKING-GLASS by Lewis Carroll
2. THE WONDERFUL WIZARD OF OZ by L. Frank Baum
3. THE HARRY POTTER SERIES by J.K. Rowling

4

FROM A RAILWAY CARRIAGE

Faster than fairies, faster than witches,
Bridges and houses, hedges and ditches;
And charging along like troops in a battle,
All through the meadows the horses
and cattle:
All of the sights of the hill and the plain
Fly as thick as driving rain;
And ever again, in the wink of an eye,
Painted stations whistle by.

Here is a child who **clambers** and scrambles,
All by himself and gathering **brambles**;
Here is a **tramp** who stands and gazes;
And there is the green for stringing
the daisies!

Here is a cart run away in the road
Lumping along with man and load;
And here is a mill and there is a river;
Each a glimpse and gone for ever!

ROBERT LOUIS STEVENSON (1850–1894) was a poet and novelist. His famous books are *A Child's Garden of Verses, Treasure Island, Kidnapped,* and *Strange Case of Dr. Jekyll and Mr. Hyde.*

WORDS TO KNOW

clambers: moves with difficulty

brambles: wild bushes with thorns

tramp: a person who moves from place to place asking people for food or money

FOR DISCUSSION

1. The poet is trying to describe a magical experience. Are there any lines in the poem that tell you that this ride is better than magic?
2. The poet never talks about the train. How does he show the speed of the train?
3. The poem uses pairs of rhyming lines. How does this help describe the train or its movement?
4. Can you find one thing in the poem which is opposite to the quick speed of the train?

LANGUAGE

Simile

The poem uses a lot of comparisons to talk about the train and the things seen from the train. From these can you identify the two similes used? (HINT: A simile is a comparison that uses the word 'like' to talk about how two things are similar.)

Describe a journey you have taken in any mode of transport, and use at least two similes to describe the way in which things move past the vehicle.

5
David Reaches Dover

I inquired about my aunt among the boatmen first, and received various answers. One said she lived in the South Foreland **Light**, and had singed her whiskers by doing so; another, that she was made fast to the great **buoy** outside the harbour, and could only be visited at half-tide; a third, that she was locked up in Maidstone jail for child-stealing; a fourth, that she was seen to mount a broom in the last high wind, and make direct for Calais.

The **fly-drivers**, among whom I inquired next, were equally disrespectful; and the shopkeepers, not liking my appearance, generally replied, without hearing what I had to say, that they had got nothing for me. I felt more miserable and destitute than I had done at any period of my running away. My money was all gone,

CHARLES DICKENS (1812–1870) was one of the greatest English novelists. Some of his well-known books are *Oliver Twist* and *David Copperfield.* This extract has been taken from the latter.

David Copperfield, a young boy whose parents have died and who has no one to care for him, sets out from London to Dover to find his father's aunt Betsey Trotwood, who has not seen him since he was a baby. David sets out from London but, after having all his money and clothes stolen, has to walk most of the way. What happens when he reaches Dover? Let's read to find out.

I had nothing left to sell; I was hungry, thirsty, and worn out; and seemed as distant from my goal as if I had remained in London.

I was sitting on the step of an empty shop at a street corner, near the marketplace, deliberating upon what to do next, when a passing fly-driver dropped a **horsecloth**. Something good-natured in the man's face, as I handed it up, encouraged me to ask him if he could tell me where Miss Trotwood lived; though I had asked the question so often, that it almost died upon my lips.

'Trotwood,' said he. 'Let me see. I know the name, too. Old lady?'

'Yes,' I said, 'rather.'

'Pretty stiff in the back?' said he, making himself upright.

'Yes,' I said. 'I should think it very likely.'

'Carries a bag?' said he. 'A bag with a good deal of room in it—is gruffish, and comes down upon you, sharp?'

My heart sank within me as I acknowledged the undoubted accuracy of this description.

'Why then, I tell you what,' said he. 'If you go up there,' pointing with his whip towards the heights, 'and keep right on till you come to some houses facing the sea, I think you'll hear of her. My opinion is she won't stand anything, so here's a penny for you.'

I accepted the gift thankfully, and bought a loaf with it. Dispatching this refreshment by the way, I went in the direction my friend had indicated, and walked on a good distance without coming to the houses he had mentioned. At length I saw some before me; and approaching them, went into a little shop (it was what we used to call a general shop, at home), and inquired if they could have the goodness to tell me where Miss Trotwood lived. I addressed myself to a man behind the counter, who was weighing some rice for a young woman who turned round quickly.

'My mistress?' she said. 'What do you want with her, boy?'

'I want,' I replied, 'to speak to her, if you please.'

'To beg of her, you mean,' retorted the damsel.

'No,' I said, 'indeed.' But suddenly remembering that in truth I came for no other purpose, I held my peace in confusion, and felt my face burn.

My aunt's handmaid, as I supposed she was from what she had said, put her rice in a little basket and walked out of the shop; telling me that I could follow her, if I wanted to know where Miss Trotwood lived. I needed no second permission; though I was by this time in such a state of consternation and agitation, that my legs shook under me. I followed the young woman, and we soon came to a very neat little cottage with cheerful bow-windows: in front of it, a small square gravelled court or garden full of flowers, carefully tended, and smelling deliciously.

'This is Miss Trotwood's,' said the young woman. 'Now you know; and that's all I have got to say.' With which words she hurried into the house, and left me standing at the garden-gate, looking disconsolately over the top of it.

My shoes were by this time in a woeful condition. The soles had shed themselves bit by bit, and the upper leathers had broken and burst until the very shape and form of shoes had departed from them. My hat (which had served me for a night-cap, too) was so crushed and bent, that no old battered handleless saucepan on a dunghill need have been ashamed to compete with it. My torn shirt and trousers, stained with heat, dew, grass, and the soil on which I had slept might have frightened the birds from my aunt's garden. My hair had known no comb or brush since I left London. My face, neck, and hands, from exposure to the air and sun, were burnt to a berry-brown. From head to foot, I was powdered almost white with dust. In this plight, and with a strong consciousness of it, I waited to make my first impression on my aunt.

After a while, deciding that she was not there, I was on the point of slinking off. There came out of the house a lady with her handkerchief tied over her cap, and a pair of gardening gloves on her hands, wearing a gardening apron, and carrying a great knife. I knew her immediately to be Miss Betsey, for she came **stalking** out of the house exactly as my poor mother had so often described her stalking up our garden.

'Go away!' said Miss Betsey, shaking her head, and making a distant chop in the air with her knife. 'No boys here!'

I watched her, with my heart at my lips, as she marched to a corner of her garden, and stooped to dig up some little root there. Then, without a scrap of courage, but with a great deal of desperation, I went softly in and stood beside her, touching her with my finger.

'If you please, ma'am,' I began.

She started and looked up.

'If you please, aunt.'

'EH?' exclaimed Miss Betsey, in a tone of amazement I have never heard approached.

'If you please, aunt, I am your nephew.'

'Oh, Lord!' said my aunt. And sat flat down in the garden-path.

WORDS TO KNOW

Light: refers to a lighthouse—a tower with a huge fire or light burning to tell ships where the land is

buoy: a large object that floats in water and is used to mark a route or location in the sea.

fly-drivers: people who drove horse-drawn wagons that functioned as taxis in the times before cars were invented

horsecloth: a cloth used to cover a horse and keep it warm

stalking: walking in a straight and stiff manner

FOR DISCUSSION

1. From the descriptions provided by the helpful driver, what do you think is the personality of Miss Betsey Trotwood?
2. The maid thinks David wants to beg from Betsey Trotwood. Why do you think that is?

3. The first few people that David asked gave him answers that made no sense or were complete lies. Why do you think these people behaved in such a way? Do you think it is because of what David looks like, or what Mrs Trotwood is like, or is it a mix of both?
4. If you were David, do you think you would have been more confident than him? Why or why not?
5. What do you think happens next in this story?

LANGUAGE

Words and phrases

The novel *David Copperfield* from which this passage is taken, was written in 1850 by Charles Dickens. That is why the language of the novel is slightly different from the English we use now. Some of these differences are because of the way the world has changed. For instance, in Dickens's time, cars and vehicles that ran on engines had not yet been invented. The most common means of fast transport in cities was a horse-drawn carriage (often called 'fly' because it was light and fast).

But some idiomatic phrases are still in use, though maybe slightly changed. Let us look at a few from the text.

almost died upon my lips: David thought of asking something but he almost did not. 'Died upon my lips' generally is used to talk about a thought that is not spoken or expressed.

comes down upon you: This expression is used by the friendly fly-driver to talk about Miss Trotwood. The expression signifies that Miss Trotwood speaks to people in a rough and scolding manner.

heart sank within me: David uses this to describe his feelings when told about his extremely strict aunt. This indicates that he felt unsure and afraid.

won't stand anything: This indicates that Miss Trotwood won't listen to anything that she doesn't like. In this case, the fly-driver probably thinks that David is a beggar child going to Miss Trotwood to ask for help or money.

held my peace: This expression is another way of saying that he kept silent and didn't say anything.

felt my face burn: This indicates that he felt ashamed or embarrassed. It is a reference to the fact that your face feels hot in this situation.

my heart at my lips: (modern version: my heart in my mouth) David uses this to talk about his feelings when he sees his aunt for the first time. He feels afraid and anxious.

Look at these words and phrases used in the story and figure out what they mean.

1. **singed:** burnt / grew / sang
2. **made fast:** ran quickly / cooked quickly / tied up
3. **destitute:** very happy / extremely poor / totally alone
4. **gruffish:** in a quiet way / in an angry way / in a polite way
5. **sharp:** quickly / slowly / quietly
6. **dispatching:** here, eating / working / meeting
7. **retorted:** replied / shouted / loved
8. **disconsolately:** excitedly / sadly / happily
9. **slinking off:** going away quietly / walking proudly away / running away excitedly

READING IDEAS

If you liked this story, you could read:

1. GREAT EXPECTATIONS by Charles Dickens
2. THE ANNE OF GREEN GABLES SERIES by L.M. Montgomery
3. MALGUDI DAYS by R.K. Narayan
4. DADDY LONG LEGS by Jean Webster
5. JANE EYRE by Charlotte Bronte

6

'HOPE' IS THE THING WITH FEATHERS

'Hope' is the thing with feathers –
That **perches** in the soul –
And sings the tune without the words
And never stops – at all –

And sweetest – in the **Gale** – is heard –
And sore must be the storm –
That could **abash the little Bird**
That kept so many warm –

I've heard it in the chillest land –
And on the strangest Sea –
Yet – never – **in Extremity**,
It asked a crumb – of me.

EMILY DICKINSON

EMILY DICKINSON (1830–1886) an American poet, wrote many poems on nature, society and life in general.

WORDS TO KNOW

perches: sits

gale: wind

abash the little Bird: shame or embarrass the little bird

in Extremity: at the end or limit

FOR DISCUSSION

1. Do you think the poet is correct in describing hope as a bird?
2. Do you agree with the poet? Does 'hope' keep you warm in troubled times?
3. This poem does not have a proper title—it uses the first line as a name. Can you think of a title for the poem that does not have the word 'hope' in it?
4. Why do you think the poet says 'the thing with feathers' rather than 'bird'?

LANGUAGE

Imagery

The poem uses the image of a bird to speak of hope. Imagery is when a poet or author creates an image or a picture of something in the minds of the reader.

1. Keeping this in mind, what do you think the 'chilliest land' and the 'gale' in the poem could be? (HINT: Like hope, these are also things that are felt in the mind.)
2. Also, can you think of another image that you could use to talk about 'hope'?

7
THE MISSING TREASURE

It was hard for me to keep up with the rapid pace of the treasure-hunters. Now and again, I stumbled, and it was then that Silver launched at me his murderous glances. Dick, who had dropped behind us and now brought up the rear, was babbling to himself as his fever kept rising. We were now at the margin of the thicket.

'Huzza, mates, all together!' shouted Merry; and the foremost broke into a run.

And suddenly, not ten yards further, we **beheld** them stop. A low cry arose. Silver doubled his pace, digging away with the foot of his crutch like one possessed; and next moment he and I had come also to a dead halt.

Before us was a great excavation, not very recent, for the sides had fallen in

ROBERT LOUIS STEVENSON (1850–1894) was a novelist and poet. His famous books are *Treasure Island, Kidnapped, Strange Case of Dr. Jekyll and Mr. Hyde,* and *A Child's Garden of Verses.*

This passage is from R.L. Stevenson's Treasure Island, *a tale narrated by a young boy, Jim Hawkins. Jim finds the map to a pirate treasure and accompanies two men of his village—the Squire and Dr Livesey—on a voyage to find the treasure. After many adventures on the island, Jim is caught by Silver and pirates. They set off with the help of the map and reach the marked spot.*

and grass had sprouted on the bottom. In this were the shaft of a pick broken in two and the boards of several packing-cases strewn around. On one of these boards I saw, branded with a hot iron, the name Walrus—the name of Flint's ship.

All was clear. The cache had been found and rifled; the seven hundred thousand pounds were gone!

There never was such an overturn in this world. Each of these six men was as though he had been struck. But with Silver the blow passed almost instantly. Every thought of his soul had been set full-stretch, like a racer, on that money; well, he was brought up, in a single second, dead; and he kept his head, found his temper, and changed his plan before the others had had time to realize the disappointment.

'Jim,' he whispered, 'take that, and stand by for trouble.' And he passed me a double-barrelled pistol.

At the same time, he began quietly moving, and in a few steps had put the hollow between us two and the other five. Then he looked at me and nodded. His looks were not quite friendly, and I was so revolted at these constant changes that I could not forbear whispering, 'So you've changed sides again.'

There was no time left for him to answer in. The buccaneers, with oaths and cries, began to leap, one after another, into the pit and to dig with their fingers, throwing the boards aside as they did so. Morgan found a piece of gold. He held it up with a perfect spout of oaths. It was a two-guinea piece, and it went from hand to hand among them for a quarter of a minute.

'Two guineas!' roared Merry, shaking it at Silver. 'That's your seven hundred thousand pounds, is it? You're the man for bargains, ain't you? You're him that never bungled nothing, you wooden-headed lubber!'

'Dig away, boys,' said Silver with the coolest insolence; 'you'll find some pig-nuts and I shouldn't wonder.'

'Pig-nuts!' repeated Merry, in a scream. 'Mates, do you hear that? I tell you now, that man there knew it all along. Look in the face of him and you'll see it wrote there.'

'Ah, Merry,' remarked Silver, 'standing for **cap'n** again? You're a pushing lad, to be sure.'

But this time everyone was entirely in Merry's favour. They began to scramble out of the excavation, darting furious glances behind them. One thing I observed, which looked well for us: they all got out upon the opposite side from Silver.

Well, there we stood, two on one side, five on the other, the pit between us, and nobody screwed up high enough to offer the first blow. Silver never moved; he watched them, very upright on his crutch, and looked as cool as ever I saw him. He was brave, and no mistake.

At last Merry seemed to think a speech might help matters.

'Mates,' says he, 'there's two of them alone there; one's the old cripple that brought us all here and blundered us down to this; the other's that cub that I mean to have the heart of. Now, mates—'

He was raising his arm and his voice, and plainly meant to lead a charge. But just then—crack! crack! crack!—three **musket**-shots flashed out of the thicket. Merry tumbled head foremost into the excavation; the man with the bandage spun round like a **teetotum** and fell all his length upon his side, where he lay dead, but still twitching; and the other three turned and ran for it with all their might.

Before you could wink, Long John had fired two barrels of a pistol into the struggling Merry, and as the man rolled up his eyes at him in the last agony, 'George,' said he, 'I reckon I settled you.'

At the same moment, the doctor, Gray, and Ben Gunn joined us, with smoking muskets, from among the trees.

'Forward!' cried the doctor. 'Double quick, my lads. We must head 'em off the boats.'

And we set off at a great pace, sometimes plunging through the bushes to the chest.

I tell you, but Silver was anxious to keep up with us. The work that man went through, leaping on his crutch till the muscles of his chest were fit to burst, was work no sound man ever equalled; and so thinks the doctor. As it was, he was already thirty yards behind us and on the verge of strangling when we reached the brow of the slope.

'Doctor,' he hailed, 'see there! No hurry!'

Sure enough, there was no hurry. In a more open part of the plateau, we could see the three survivors still running in the same direction as they had started, right for Mizzenmast Hill. We were already between them and the boats; and so we four sat down to breathe, while Long John, mopping his face, came slowly up with us.

'Thank ye kindly, doctor,' says he. 'You **came in in about the nick**, I guess, for me and Hawkins. And so it's you, Ben Gunn!' he added. 'Well, you're a nice one, to be sure.'

The doctor sent back Gray for one of the pick-axes deserted, in their flight, by the mutineers, and then as we proceeded leisurely downhill to where the boats were lying, related in a few words what had taken place. It was a story that profoundly interested Silver; and Ben Gunn was the hero from beginning to end.

Ben, in his long, lonely wanderings about the island, had found the treasure. He had dug it up (it was the **haft** of his pick-axe that lay broken in the excavation). He had carried it on his back, in many weary journeys, from the foot of the tall pine to a cave he had on the two-pointed hill at the north-east angle of the island, and there it had lain stored in safety since two months before the arrival of the *Hispaniola.*

But, that morning, finding that I was to be involved in the horrid disappointment he had prepared for the mutineers, the doctor had run all the way to the cave, and leaving the squire to guard the captain, had taken

Gray and Ben Gunn and travelled across the island to be at hand beside the pine. Gray and the doctor had been ready and hidden before the arrival of the treasure-hunters.

'Ah,' said Silver, 'it were fortunate for me that I had Hawkins here. You would have let old John be cut to bits, and never given it a thought, doctor.'

'Not a thought,' replied Dr. Livesey cheerily.

WORDS TO KNOW

beheld: saw

cap'n: captain

musket: old type of long gun

teetotum: a type of spinning top

came in in about the nick: came at the right time

haft: handle

FOR DISCUSSION

1. Why do you think Silver quickly changes sides when he discovers the empty treasure spot?
2. Jim does not trust Silver because he keeps changing sides depending on where the advantage lies. Do you think you would have trusted Silver?
3. Silver was so anxious to keep up with the others that he made an almost superhuman effort. Why do you think he was so anxious to stay with them?
4. What does Dr Livesey's last line in the text tell you about what he thinks of Silver?

5. Do you think you are a quick thinker like Silver? How would you have felt in his situation?

LANGUAGE

Let's take a look at some of the words and phrases used in the text and guess what they mean.

1. **branded:** named / called / marked
2. **cache had been rifled:** the money had been stolen / the coins had been attacked / the notes had holes in them
3. **buccaneers:** beggars / adventurers / pirates
4. **insolence:** politeness / calmness / rudeness
5. **pushing:** rude / ambitious / quick
6. **hailed:** shouted / laughed / praised
7. **lead a charge:** push others ahead / start an attack / talk for a while

Let's take a look at some of the idiomatic expressions and what they mean, to understand how they can be used in everyday conversations.

screwed up high enough: brave enough or angry enough

before you could wink: extremely quickly

to be at hand: to be very near

Can you think of any situations in which these could be used in a conversation?

READING IDEAS

If you liked this story, you could read:

1. STRANGE CASE OF DR. JEKYLL AND MR. HYDE by R.L. Stevenson
2. ROBINSON CRUSOE by Daniel Defoe
3. THE ADVENTURES OF TOM SAWYER by Mark Twain

8

THE COMIC SONG

We were a fashionable and very intelligent party. We had on our best clothes, and we talked much, and were very happy—all except two young fellows, students, just returned from Germany, ordinary young men, who seemed restless and uncomfortable. The truth was, I expect, that we were too clever for them. They did not understand our brilliant conversation, they were out of place amongst us. They ought never to have been there at all. Everybody agreed about that, later.

We had music by the old German masters. We discussed life and ideals. Somebody recited a French poem after supper, and we said it was beautiful, and then a lady sang a love song in Spanish, and it made one or two of us weep—it was so sad.

And then those two young men got up, and asked us if we had ever heard Herr

JEROME K. JEROME (1859–1927) was an English writer, best known for *Three Men in a Boat* from which this extract has been taken.

Three Men in a Boat *is widely regarded as one of the wittiest classics ever written. Three friends set out on a two-week boating holiday with their dog. The book describes their journey on the river Thames and their adventures in the course of the journey. This excerpt is about how the friends think that a certain German song is a comic one. What happens next?*

Slossenn Boschen (who had just arrived, and was then down in the supper room) sing his great German comic song.

None of us had heard it, that we could remember. The young men said that it was the funniest song that had ever been written, and that, if we liked, they would persuade Herr Slossenn Boschen, whom they knew well, to sing it. They said it was so funny, that, when Herr Slossenn Boschen had sung it once before the German Emperor, he (the German Emperor) had had to be carried to bed. They said nobody could sing it like Herr Slossenn Boschen, he was so serious all through it that you might fancy he was reciting a tragedy, and that, of course, made it all the funnier.

We said that we were very eager to hear it, that we wanted a good laugh, and they went downstairs, and fetched Herr Slossenn Boschen. He appeared to be quite pleased to sing it, for he came up at once, and sat down at the piano without a word.

'Oh, it will amuse you. You will laugh,' whispered the two young men, as they passed through the room, and took up a position behind the Professor's back.

Herr Slossenn Boschen played the piano himself. The introduction did not suggest a comic song exactly. It was strangely sad. It quite made one's flesh creep, but we murmured to one another that it was the German method, and prepared to enjoy it.

I don't understand German myself. I learned it at school, but forgot every word of it two years after I had left, and have felt much better ever since. Still, I did not want the people there to guess my ignorance.

So, I hit upon what I thought to be rather a good idea. I kept my eye on the two young students, and followed them. When they smiled, I smiled, when they roared, I roared, and I also put in a laugh all by myself now and then, as if I had seen something funny that had escaped the others, I considered this particularly clever on my part.

I noticed, as the song progressed, that a good many other people seemed to have their eye fixed on the two young men also. These other people also smiled when the young men smiled, and roared when the young men roared, and, as the two young men smiled and roared and exploded with laughter almost continuously all through the song, it went exceedingly well.

And yet that German Professor did not seem happy. At first, when we began to laugh the expression on his face was one of great surprise, as if laughter were the very last thing he had expected to be greeted with. We thought this very funny we said that his solemn manner was half the humour.

As we continued to laugh his surprise changed to an air of anger, and he scowled fiercely round upon us all (except upon the two young men who, being behind him, he could not see). That made us laugh all the more. We told each other that this would kill us. The words alone, we said, were enough to make us burst, but added to his pretended seriousness—oh. It was too much.

He finished amid a perfect shriek of laughter. We said it was the funniest thing we had ever heard in all our lives. And we asked the Professor why he didn't translate the song into English, so that the common people could understand it and hear what a real comic song was like.

Then Herr Slossenn Boschen got up, and completely lost his temper. He swore at us in German, and he danced, and shook his fists, and called us **all the English he knew**. He said that he had never been so insulted in all his life.

It appeared that the song was not a comic song at all. It was about a young girl who lived in the Hartz Mountains, and who had given up her life to save her lover's soul, and he died, and met her spirit in the air, and then, in the last verse, he left her—I'm not quite sure of the details, but it was something very sad, I know. Herr Boschen said it was generally considered to be one of the most tragic songs in the German language.

It was a very difficult situation for us all. There seemed to be nothing we could say. We looked round for the two young men who had done this thing, but they had left the house as quietly as possible immediately after the end of the song.

That was the end of the party. We never said good-night even to one another. We came downstairs one at a time, walking softly. We asked the servant for our hats and coats in whispers, opened the door for ourselves, slipped out, and got round the corner quickly, avoiding each other as much as possible. I have never taken much interest in German songs since then.

WORDS TO KNOW

all the English he knew: shows that he knew very little English

FOR DISCUSSION

1. Do you agree with the narrator that the two young men should not have been there?
2. How do you think Herr Slossenn Boschen must have felt when the people laughed?
3. Would you have done the same as the narrator?
4. Why do you think the two young men behaved in such a manner?
5. Have you ever experienced a situation where you might have been in the position of either Herr Slossenn Boschen or the audience?

LANGUAGE

Can you guess the correct meaning of the following words from the story?

1. **fancy:** imagine / like / find
2. **roared:** laughed politely / laughed loudly / laughed quietly

Idiomatic expressions

The narrator uses an idiomatic expression to talk about the effect of Herr Slossenn Boschen's song on the people listening. He says that it **made one's flesh creep**. This expression usually shows that the person was horrified or made uncomfortable by something.

Now see if you can guess what these expressions mean:

1. made one's hair stand on end
2. gave one the heebie-jeebies
3. made one's blood run cold
4. made one jump out of one's skin

Narrative technique

When the author tells us the story, right at the beginning he says, 'They ought never to have been there at all. Everybody agreed about that, later.' This line tells us what's going to happen after the party. This is an example of a technique in story-writing called 'foreshadowing'. Here, the author gives us a hint about something that is going to happen. The reader already knows that the young men are important, and that there is a surprise at the end.

When you read the text, do you feel you know what is going to happen next?

READING IDEAS

If you liked this story, you could read:

1. THE JEEVES SERIES by P.G. Wodehouse
2. THE RUSTY SERIES by Ruskin Bond

9

THE QUANGLE WANGLE'S HAT

On the top of the Crumpetty Tree
The Quangle Wangle sat,
But his face you could not see,
On account of his Beaver Hat.
For his Hat was a hundred and two feet wide,
With ribbons and bibbons on every side
And bells, and buttons, and loops, and lace,
So that nobody ever could see the face
Of the Quangle Wangle Quee.

The Quangle Wangle said
To himself on the Crumpetty Tree, –
'Jam; and jelly; and bread;
'Are the best of food for me!
'But the longer I live on this Crumpetty Tree
'The plainer than ever it seems to me
'That very few people come this way
'And that life on the whole is far from gay!'
Said the Quangle Wangle Quee.

But there came to the Crumpetty Tree,
Mr. and Mrs. Canary;
And they said, – 'Did ever you see
'Any spot so charmingly airy?
'May we build a nest on your lovely Hat?
'Mr. Quangle Wangle, grant us that!
'O please let us come and build a nest
'Of whatever material suits you best,
'Mr. Quangle Wangle Quee!'

And besides, to the Crumpetty Tree
Came the Stork, the Duck, and the Owl;
The Snail, and the Bumble-Bee,
The Frog, and the Fimble Fowl;
(The Fimble Fowl, with a corkscrew leg;)
And all of them said, – 'We humbly beg,
'We may build out homes on your lovely Hat, –
'Mr. Quangle Wangle, grant us that!
'Mr. Quangle Wangle Quee!'

And the Golden Grouse came there,
And the Pobble who has no toes, –
And the small Olympian bear, –
And the Dong with a luminous nose.
And the Blue Baboon, who played the Flute, –
And the Orient Calf from the Land of Tute, –
And the Attery Squash, and the Bisky Bat, –

All came and built on the lovely Hat
Of the Quangle Wangle Quee.
And the Quangle Wangle said
To himself on the Crumpetty Tree, –
'When all these creatures move
'What a wonderful noise there'll be!'
And at night by the light of the Mulberry moon
They danced to the Flute of the Blue Baboon,
On the broad green leaves of the Crumpetty Tree,
And all were as happy as happy could be,
With the Quangle Wangle Quee.

EDWARD LEAR (1812–1888) was a British poet, writer, illustrator and musician known mostly for his nonsense verse.

READING IDEAS

1. The poet uses a lot of unusual names for imaginary creatures—the Quangle Wangle Quee, the Pobble, the Fimble Fowl, the Attery Squash, and so on. Does it confuse you, or does it sound magical and interesting?
2. Do you think the Quangle Wangle is a friendly creature?
3. What do you think the Quangle Wangle or the other mysterious creatures mentioned in the poem look like?

LANGUAGE

Nonsense verse

This is a style of poem known as nonsense verse. The poem talks about people or things that may not actually exist in real life. Nonsense verse can have unusual or imaginary people, things, animals and incidents. In addition, nonsense verse often has invented or meaningless words.

1. Find the invented words in the poem. (You can use a dictionary if you are not sure which words are invented.)
2. Try and imagine an animal, plant or bird which does not exist in the real world. Describe and name it. Make sure the name is an unusual one.
3. You can find many more examples of nonsense verse by the poet Edward Lear. Similar poems can also be found in the books of Lewis Carroll, especially the poem 'Jabberwocky'.

10
Nat Comes to Plumfield

'Please, sir, is this Plumfield?' asked a ragged boy of the man who opened the great gate at which the **omnibus** left him.

'Yes. Who sent you?'

'Mr Laurence. I have got a letter for the lady.'

'All right. Go up to the house, and give it to her. She'll see to you, little chap.'

The man spoke pleasantly, and the boy went on, feeling much cheered by the words. Through the soft spring rain that fell on sprouting grass and budding trees, Nat saw a large square house before him—a hospitable-looking house, with an old-fashioned **porch**, wide steps, and lights shining in many windows. Neither curtains nor shutters hid the cheerful glimmer; and, pausing a moment before he rang, Nat saw many little shadows dancing on the walls,

LOUISA MAY ALCOTT (1832–1888), best known for her novel *Little Women,* was an American writer.

Little Women *was followed by two sequels* Little Men *and* Jo's Boys. *This excerpt is from* Little Men. *Plumfield is a school run by Aunt Jo and her husband, Professor Bhaer. Nat Blake is an orphan who attends Plumfield with several other boys and girls. This particular piece is the first chapter of the book when Nat arrives at Plumfield for the first time.*

heard the pleasant hum of young voices, and felt that it was hardly possible that the light and warmth and comfort within could be for a homeless 'little chap' like him.

'I hope the lady will see to me,' he thought; and gave a timid rap with the great bronze knocker.

A rosy-faced servant-maid opened the door, and smiled as she took the letter which he silently offered. She seemed used to receiving strange boys, for she pointed to a seat in the hall, and said, with a nod: 'Sit there and drip on the mat a bit, while I take this in to missis.'

Nat found plenty to amuse him while he waited, and stared about him curiously, enjoying the view, yet glad to do so unobserved in the dusky recess by the door.

The house seemed swarming with boys, who were beguiling the rainy twilight with all sorts of amusements. There were boys everywhere, 'up-stairs and down-stairs and in the lady's chamber', apparently, for various open doors showed pleasant groups of big boys, little boys, and middle-sized boys in all stages of evening relaxation, not to say effervescence. Two large rooms on the right were evidently school-rooms, for desks, maps, blackboards, and books were scattered about. An open fire burned on the hearth, and several indolent lads lay on their backs before it, discussing a new cricket-ground, with such animation that their boots waved in the air. A tall youth was practising on the flute in one corner, quite undisturbed by the racket all about him. Two or three others were jumping over the desks, pausing, now and then, to get their breath and laugh at the droll sketches of a little **wag** who was **caricaturing** the whole household on a blackboard.

In the room on the left a long supper-table was seen, set forth with great pitchers of new milk, piles of brown and white bread, and perfect stacks of the shiny gingerbread so dear to boyish souls. A flavour of toast was in the air, also suggestions of baked apples, very tantalizing to one hungry little nose and stomach.

The hall, however, presented the most inviting prospect of all, for a fast game of tag was going on in the upper entry. One landing was devoted to marbles, the other to checkers, while the stairs were occupied by a boy reading, a girl singing a lullaby to her doll, two puppies, a kitten, and a constant succession of small boys sliding down the banisters, to the great detriment of their clothes and danger to their limbs.

So absorbed did Nat become in this exciting race, that he ventured farther and farther out of his corner; and when one very lively boy came down so swiftly that he could not stop himself, but fell off the banisters, with a crash that would have broken any head but one made nearly as hard as a cannon-ball by eleven years of constant bumping, Nat forgot himself, and ran up to the fallen rider, expecting to find him half-dead. The boy, however, only winked rapidly for a second, then lay calmly looking up at the new face with a surprised 'Hullo!'

'Hullo!' returned Nat, not knowing what else to say, and thinking that form of reply brief and easy.

'Are you a new boy?' asked the recumbent youth, without moving.

'Don't know yet.'

'What's your name?'

'Nat Blake.'

'Mine's Tommy Bangs; come up and have a go, will you?' and Tommy got up like one suddenly remembering the duties of hospitality.

'Guess I won't, till I see whether I'm going to stay or not,' returned Nat, feeling the desire to stay increase every moment.

'I say, Demi, here's a new one. Come and see to him,' and the lively Thomas returned to his sport with unabated relish.

At his call, the boy reading on the stairs looked up with a pair of big brown eyes, and after an instant's pause, as if a little shy, he put the book under his arm, and came soberly down to greet the new-comer, who found something very attractive in the pleasant face of this slender, mild-eyed boy.

'Have you seen Aunt Jo?' he asked, as if that was some sort of important ceremony.

'I haven't seen anybody yet but you boys. I'm waiting,' answered Nat.

'Did Uncle Laurie send you?' proceeded Demi, politely, but gravely.

'Mr Laurence did.'

'He is Uncle Laurie; and he always sends nice boys.'

Nat looked gratified at the remark, and smiled, in a way that made his thin face very pleasant. He did not know what to say next, so the two stood staring at one another in friendly silence, till the little girl came up with her doll in her arms.

She was very like Demi, only not so tall, and had a rounder, rosier face, and blue eyes.

'This is my sister Daisy,' announced Demi, as if presenting a rare and precious creature.

The children nodded to one another; and the little girl's face dimpled with pleasure, as she said affably: 'I hope you'll stay. We have such good times here. Don't we, Demi?'

'Of course, we do; that's what Aunt Jo has Plumfield for.'

'It seems a very nice place indeed,' observed Nat, feeling that he must respond to these amiable young persons.

'It's the nicest place in the world. Isn't it, Demi?' said Daisy, who evidently regarded her brother as an authority on all subjects.

'No, I think Greenland, where the icebergs and seals are, is more interesting. But I'm fond of Plumfield, and it is a very nice place to be in,' returned

Demi, who was interested just now in a book on Greenland. He was about to offer to show Nat the pictures and explain them, when the servant returned, saying, with a nod toward the parlour-door: 'All right; you are to stop.'

'I'm glad. Now come to Aunt Jo.' And Daisy took him by the hand with a pretty protecting air, which made Nat feel at home at once.

WORDS TO KNOW

omnibus: (old use) a large bus carrying many passengers

porch: a covered area in front of the entrance of a house

wag: (old use) a person who makes jokes

caricaturing: making funny pictures

FOR DISCUSSION

1. Nat is a homeless boy who has come to a large house full of young children. Read the story to see how Nat feels about the place.
2. Do you think Nat has come to a place where there are strict rules?
3. What do you think the place is where Nat has arrived?
4. Who do you think Aunt Jo is in Plumfield?
5. Do you think Nat will be comfortable in Plumfield? Why do you think so?

LANGUAGE

Let's take a look at some of the words and phrases used in the story and try to figure out their meanings. Read the text again to find the meaning.

1. **a timid rap:** a loud sound / a soft knock / a hard thud
2. **dusky recess:** dirty space / empty area / dark space
3. **beguiling:** fooling / spending / making
4. **indolent:** lazy / rude / silent
5. **droll:** strange / bad / funny
6. **inviting prospect:** attractive sight / beautiful place / crowded area
7. **absorbed:** completely interested / completely ignoring / completely confused by
8. **recumbent:** standing up / sleeping / lying down
9. **unabated:** not reduced / not happy / not the same
10. **to the great detriment of:** having no effect on / having little effect on / having a bad effect on

Comparisons

The author notes that Tommy Bangs's head was 'as hard as a cannon-ball'. This simile uses 'as ... as' to compare two things.

Can you think of more similes that you use in everyday life to describe people or things? Think of the instances where you could use the following: as timid as a mouse, as hard as a rock, as cold as ice, as playful as a puppy, as quick as thought, and so on.

READING IDEAS

If you liked this story, you could read:

1. LITTLE WOMEN by Louisa May Alcott
2. WHAT KATY DID by Susan Coolidge

11

LILLIPUT AND ITS LAWS

JONATHAN SWIFT (1667–1745), an Irish writer who wrote many essays, short stories, poems, was best known for his book *Gulliver's Travels*.

The narrator of this story, Gulliver, sets out on a long sea voyage. His ship is wrecked in a storm and he wakes up on an island. The people on this island, named Lilliput, are tiny beings, about six inches tall on an average. He is a giant for them. He lives among them for a while, noting some interesting things about them, like the interesting laws of the land, which he presents as a contrast to the laws of England.

Although I intend to leave the description of this empire to a particular treatise, yet, in the meantime, I am content to gratify the curious reader with some general ideas. As the common size of the natives is somewhat under six inches high, so there is an exact proportion in all other animals, as well as plants and trees: for instance, the tallest horses and oxen are between four and five inches in height, the sheep an inch and half, more or less: their geese about the bigness of a sparrow, and so the several gradations downwards till you come to the smallest, which to my sight, were almost invisible; but nature has adapted the eyes of the Lilliputians to all objects proper for their view: they see with great exactness, but at no great distance. And, to show the sharpness of their sight towards objects that are near, I have been much pleased with observing a young girl threading an invisible needle with invisible silk. Their tallest trees are about seven feet high: I mean some of those in the great royal park, the tops **whereof** I could but just reach with my fist clenched. The other vegetables are in the same proportion; but this I leave to the reader's imagination.

And here it may, perhaps, divert the curious reader, to give some account of my manner of living in this country, during a residence of nine months, and thirteen days. Having a head mechanically turned, and being likewise forced by necessity, I had made for myself a table and chair convenient enough, out of the largest trees in the royal park. Two hundred **sempstresses** were employed to make me shirts, and linen for my bed and

table, all of the strongest and coarsest kind they could get; which, however, they were forced to quilt together in several folds, for the thickest was some degrees finer than **lawn**. Their linen is usually three inches wide, and three feet make a piece. The sempstresses took my measure as I lay on the ground, one standing at my neck, and another at my mid-leg, with a strong cord extended, that each held by the end, while a third measured the length of the cord with a rule of an inch long. Then they measured my right thumb, and desired no more; for by a mathematical computation, that twice round the thumb is once round the wrist, and so on to the neck and the waist, and by the help of my old shirt, which I displayed on the ground before them for a pattern, they fitted me exactly. Three hundred tailors were employed in the same manner to make me clothes; but they had another contrivance for taking my measure. I kneeled down, and they raised a ladder from the ground to my neck; upon this ladder one of them mounted, and let fall a plumb-line from my collar to the floor, which just answered the length of my coat: but my waist and arms I measured myself. When my clothes were finished, which was done in my house (for the largest of theirs would not have been able to hold them), they looked like the patch-work made by the ladies in England, only that mine were all of a colour.

There are some laws and customs in this empire very peculiar; and if they were not so directly contrary to those of my own dear country, I should be tempted to say a little in their justification. It is only to be wished they were as well executed. The first I shall mention, relates to informers. All crimes against the state are punished here with the utmost severity; but, if the person accused makes his innocence plainly to appear upon his trial, the accuser is immediately put to an ignominious death; and out of his goods or lands the innocent person is quadruply recompensed for the loss of his time, for the danger he underwent, for the hardship of his imprisonment, and for all the charges he has been at in making his defence; or, if that fund be deficient, it is largely supplied by the crown. The emperor also confers on him some public mark of his favour, and proclamation is made of his innocence through the whole city.

They look upon fraud as a greater crime than theft, and therefore seldom fail to punish it with death; for they allege, that care and vigilance, with a very common understanding, may preserve a man's goods from thieves, but honesty has no defence against superior cunning. And, since it is necessary that there should be a perpetual intercourse of buying and selling, and dealing upon credit, where fraud is permitted and connived at, or has no law to punish it, the honest dealer is always undone, and the knave gets the advantage. I remember, when I was once interceding with the emperor for a criminal who had wronged his master of a great sum of money, which he had received by order and ran away with; and happening to tell his majesty, by way of extenuation, that it was only a breach of trust, the emperor thought it monstrous in me to offer as a defence the greatest aggravation of the crime; and truly I had little to say in return, farther than the common answer, that different nations had different customs; for, I confess, I was heartily ashamed.

Although we usually call reward and punishment the two hinges upon which all government turns, yet I could never observe this maxim to be put in practice by any nation except that of Lilliput. Whoever can there bring sufficient proof, that he has strictly observed the laws of his country for seventy-three moons, has a claim to certain privileges, according to his quality or condition of life, with a proportionable sum of money out of a fund appropriated for that use: he likewise acquires the title of snilpall, or legal, which is added to his name, but does not descend to his posterity.

And these people thought it a prodigious defect of policy among us, when I told them that our laws were enforced only by penalties, without any mention of reward. It is upon this account that the image of Justice, in their courts of judicature, is formed with six eyes, two before, as many behind, and on each side one, to signify circumspection; with a bag of gold open in her right hand, and a sword sheathed in her left, to show she is more disposed to reward than to punish.

In choosing persons for all employments, they have more regard to good morals than to great abilities; for, since government is necessary to mankind, they believe, that the common size of human understanding is fitted to some station or other; and that Providence never intended to make the management of public affairs a mystery to be comprehended only by a few persons of sublime genius, of which there seldom are three born in an age: but they suppose truth, justice, temperance, and the like, to be in every man's power; the practice of which virtues, assisted by experience and a good intention, would qualify any man for the service of his country, except where a course of study is required.

But they thought the want of moral virtues was so far from being supplied by superior endowments of the mind, that employments could never be put into such dangerous hands as those of persons so qualified; and, at least, that the mistakes committed by ignorance, in a virtuous disposition, would never be of such fatal consequence to the public weal, as the practices of a man, whose inclinations led him to be corrupt, and who had great abilities to manage, to multiply, and defend his corruptions.

WORDS TO KNOW

whereof: (old use) of which

sempstresses: (old use) women who stitch clothes

lawn: very fine and soft cloth made of cotton

FOR DISCUSSION

1. How would you have felt to be one of the people of Lilliput faced with a giant like Gulliver?
2. To Gulliver, even the roughest cloth of Lilliput feels like smooth silk. How would Gulliver's clothes appear to the Lilliputians?
3. Gulliver declares that the laws of Lilliput appear to be directly contrary to that of his own country. In your opinion, which laws appear better—those of Lilliput or those of England?
4. What do you think of the Lilliputian idea of not just punishing the wrong, but rewarding the right?
5. In Lilliput, people are chosen for government not on the basis of intelligence, but on the basis of experience and possessing moral virtues. Do you think this is an idea that should be implemented everywhere?
6. If there was a new law that you would like to implement, what would it be? Remember, this should be a law that promotes equal justice.

LANGUAGE

Let's take a look at some of the words and phrases used in the text to figure out their meanings.

1. **gratify:** make happy / make angry / make curious
2. **ignominious:** easy / shameful / strange

3. **divert:** mislead / distract / entertain
4. **contrivance:** a stupid plan / a strange method / a good scheme
5. **monstrous:** fantastic / shocking / huge
6. **the greatest aggravation:** the most terrible part / the most complicated part / the best part
7. **prodigious:** strange / good / huge
8. **endowments:** here, ideas / talents / riches

Idiomatic expressions

The following idiomatic expressions are used in the text. Look at their meanings and think about the circumstances in which you could use these expressions.

1. **mechanically turned:** (the modern phrase is 'mechanically inclined') used to refer to a person who likes to make or do things with their hands
2. **connived at:** plotted or planned together with
3. **by way of extenuation:** as a partial excuse for something

READING IDEAS

If you liked this story, you could read:

1. AROUND THE WORLD IN EIGHTY DAYS by Jules Verne
2. THE THREE MUSKETEERS by Alexandre Dumas

12
HARD LUCK

Ain't no use as I can see
In sittin' underneath a tree
An' growlin' that your luck is bad,
An' that your life is extry sad;
Your life ain't sadder than your neighbor's
Nor any harder are your labors;
It rains on him the same as you,
An' he has work he hates to do;
An' he gits tired an' he gits cross,
An' he has trouble with the boss;
You take his whole life, through an' through,
Why, he's no better off than you.

If whinin' brushed the clouds away
I wouldn't have a word to say;
If it made good friends out o' foes
I'd whine a bit, too, I suppose;

But when I look around an' see
A lot o' men resemblin' me,
An' see 'em sad, an' see 'em gay
With work t' do **most** every day,
Some full o' fun, some bent with care,
Some havin' troubles hard to bear,
I reckon, as I count my woes,
They're 'bout what everybody knows.

The day I find a man who'll say
He's never known a rainy day,
Who'll raise his right hand up an' swear
In forty years he's had no care,
Has never had a single blow,
An' never known one touch o' woe,
Has never seen a loved one die,
Has never wept or heaved a sigh,
Has never had a plan go wrong,
But **allas** laughed his way along;
Then I'll sit down an' start to whine
That all the hard luck here is mine.

Edgar Albert Guest (1881–1959) was an American poet, who wrote many inspirational poems.

READING IDEAS

most: here, almost

allas: always

FOR DISCUSSION

1. Do you think 'Hard Luck' is an appropriate title for the poem? What alternate titles could it have?
2. Would you agree with the speaker when he says the following?

   Ain't no use as I can see
   In sittin' underneath a tree
   An' growlin' that your luck is bad,
   An' that your life is extry sad
3. Do you think that there might be a person who has 'never known a rainy day'?
4. The poem uses a different style of English—with missing letters, and unusual spellings—to show how English was spoken in rural America. Read the poem aloud trying to pronounce the words as they are written to know how it would sound.
5. Another effect the English used here creates is that of a song. Do you think that the poem sounds like a song when you recite it out aloud?

LANGUAGE

Imagery

The poem uses the imagery of clouds and rain to talk about troubles or sadness. This is because in England, rainy days are generally gloomy and quite cold. In India, we are more likely to look upon a rainy day with joy, especially after a long, hot summer.

What other nature imagery do you think you could use to talk about troubles or sadness? (HINT: Think of a season or weather when it is uncomfortable.)

13
THE MYSTERY OF THE TEST PAPERS

Mr Soames was a tall, **spare** man, of a nervous and excitable temperament. He was in such a state of uncontrollable agitation that it was clear something very unusual had occurred.

'Mr Holmes, we have had a very painful incident at St. Luke's. Tomorrow is the first day of the examination for the Fortescue Scholarship. I am one of the examiners. My subject is Greek, and the first of the papers consists of a large passage of Greek translation.

'The paper was lying in my room when I was in class. When I returned, though, I was aware that someone had **rummaged** among them. The paper was in three long sheets. I had left them all together. Now, I found that one of them was lying on the floor, one was on the side table near the window, and the third was where I had left it.

Sir Arthur Conan Doyle (1859–1930) was a British writer and physician. He is most known for his Sherlock Holmes stories.

Our story opens with Mr Soames, a college teacher, coming to visit the detective Sherlock Holmes and his friend Dr Watson. Dr Watson narrates the story.

'I made a most careful examination of the room. On the table in the window were several shreds from a pencil which had been sharpened. A broken tip of lead was lying there also. This was not all. I have a new writing-table with a fine surface of red leather. I found a clean cut in it about three inches long. Not only this, but on the table, I found a small ball of black dough or clay, with specks of something which looks like sawdust in it.'

Holmes is interested in this case, and they travel to Mr Soames's college to investigate the matter.

The room of our client opened by a long, low, latticed window on to the ancient courtyard of the old college. A huge arched door led to a stone staircase. On the ground floor was the tutor's room. Above were three students, one on each story. It was already twilight when we reached the scene of our problem. Holmes halted and looked earnestly at the window. Then he approached it, and, standing on tiptoe with his neck craned, he looked into the room.

Holmes enters the room to check the scene. Holmes carefully observes the table on which the papers lay and notes a few interesting things.

'He wrote so furiously that he broke his pencil, and had, as you observe, to sharpen it again. The pencil was not an ordinary one. It was above the usual size, with a soft lead, the outer colour was dark blue, the maker's name was printed in silver lettering. Look for such a pencil, Mr Soames, and you have got your man.

'Now, this small pellet is, I presume, the black, doughy mass you spoke of. Roughly pyramidal in shape and hollowed out, I perceive. As you say, there appear to be grains of sawdust in it. Dear me, this is very interesting. And the cut—a positive tear, I see. It began with a thin scratch and ended in a jagged hole. I am much indebted to you for directing my attention to this case, Mr Soames. Where does that door lead to?'

'To my bedroom.'

'Have you been in it since your adventure?'

'No, I came straight away for you.'

'I should like to have a glance round. What about this curtain?'

The drawn curtain disclosed nothing but three or four suits of clothes hanging from a line of pegs. Holmes turned away, and stooped suddenly to the floor.

'Halloa! What's this?' said he.

It was a small pyramid of black, putty-like stuff, exactly like the one upon the table of the study. Holmes held it out on his open palm in the glare of the light.

'Your visitor seems to have left **traces** in your bedroom as well as in your sitting-room, Mr Soames.'

'What could he have wanted there?'

'I think it is clear enough. You came back by an unexpected way, and so he had no warning until you were at the very door. What could he do? He caught up everything which would betray him, and he rushed into your bedroom to conceal himself.'

Holmes, Watson and Soames then go to meet each of the three students who live in the same building, all of whom were to appear for the test. The first is Gilchrist, a tall young man who is also a long-jumper. The second student is the Indian youngster, Daulat, who is shorter than the athletic Gilchrist. Daulat appears unhappy at being disturbed. While meeting both students, Holmes seems to break his pencil and asks for a replacement from them. The third student, McLaren, only shouts through the door that he won't be disturbed because he needs to study. Soames reveals that McLaren is his chief suspect as he has hardly studied through the year. Holmes inquires about McLaren's height and is told by Soames that he is of average height. After this, they return to Soames' room.

Holmes said, 'Now, Soames, I am going to ask you to have the great kindness to go up to the room of young Gilchrist, and to ask him to step down into yours.'

The tutor returned with Gilchrist. He was tall, lithe, and agile, with a springy step and a pleasant, open face. His blue eyes glanced at each of us.

'Just close the door,' said Holmes. 'Now, Mr Gilchrist, we are all quite alone here. We can be perfectly frank with each other. We want to know, Mr Gilchrist, how you, an honourable man, ever came to commit such an action as that of yesterday?'

The unfortunate young man staggered back with a look full of horror. For a moment Gilchrist, with upraised hand, tried to control his writhing features. The next he had thrown himself on his knees beside the table and, burying his face in his hands, he had burst into a storm of passionate sobbing.

'Come, come,' said Holmes, kindly, 'it is human to err. Perhaps it would be easier for you if I were to tell Mr Soames what occurred, and you can check me where I am wrong. Shall I do so?'

Holmes proceeded, 'From the moment, Mr Soames, that you said to me that no one could have told that the papers were in your room, the case

began to take a definite shape in my mind. The man who entered knew that the papers were there. But how did he know?

'When I approached your room, I examined the window. I was measuring how tall a man would need to be to see as he passed what papers were on the central table. I am six feet high, and I could do it with an effort. No one shorter than that would have a chance. Already you see I had reason to think that if one of your three students was a man of unusual height, he was the most worth watching.

'I entered and of the table I could make nothing, until in your description of Gilchrist you mentioned that he was a long-distance jumper. Then the whole thing came to me in an instant.

'What happened was this. This young fellow had been practising the jump at the athletic grounds. He returned carrying his jumping shoes, which are provided, as you are aware, with several sharp spikes. As he passed your window, he saw these papers upon your table and conjectured what they were. No harm would have been done had it not been that as he passed your door, he perceived the key which had been left by the carelessness of your servant. A sudden impulse came over him to enter and see if they were indeed the papers. It was not a dangerous exploit, for he could always pretend that he had simply looked in to ask a question.

'Well, when he saw that they were indeed the papers, it was then that he yielded to temptation. He put his shoes on the table. He took the papers, sheet by sheet, to copy them. He thought the tutor must return by the main gate, and that he would see him. As we know, he came back by the side gate. Suddenly he heard him at the very door. There was no possible escape. He caught up his shoes and darted into the bedroom.

'You observe that the scratch on that table is slight at one side, but deepens in the direction of the bedroom door. That in itself is enough to show us that the shoe had been drawn in that direction and that the culprit had taken refuge there. The earth round the spike had been left on the table, and a second sample was loosened and fell in the bedroom. I may add that I walked out to the athletic grounds this morning, saw that tenacious black clay is used in the jumping-pit, and carried away a specimen of it, together with some of the fine tan or sawdust which is strewn over it to prevent the athlete from slipping. Have I told the truth, Mr. Gilchrist?'

The student had drawn himself erect.

'Yes, sir, it is true,' said he.

'Good heavens, have you nothing to add?' cried Soames.

'Yes, sir, I have, but the shock of this disgraceful exposure has bewildered me. I have a letter here, Mr. Soames, which I wrote to you early this morning in the middle of a restless night. It was before I knew that my sin had found me out. Here it is, sir. You will see that I have said, "I have determined not to go in for the examination. I have been offered a commission in the Rhodesian Police, and I am going out to South Africa at once."'

'I am indeed pleased to hear that,' said Soames. 'But why did you change your purpose?'

Gilchrist said, 'I came to realise that I could not profit by such a deed.'

'No, indeed,' said Holmes, heartily, springing to his feet. 'Well, Soames, I think we have cleared your little problem up, and our breakfast awaits us at home. Come, Watson! As to you, sir, I trust that a bright future awaits you in Rhodesia. For once you have fallen low. Let us see, in the future, how high you can rise.'

WORDS TO KNOW

spare: thin

rummaged: moved things around to look for something

traces: small signs

FOR DISCUSSION

1. Were you able to form some idea of the culprit when reading the first part of the story?
2. Do you think Mr Soames could have made the same deductions about the culprit as Holmes?
3. What do you think Holmes would have found out by visiting the students?
4. Before Holmes reveals the culprit, were you able to guess who it was? What were the clues?

LANGUAGE

Guess the meaning of the following phrases from the story.

1. **agitation:** restlessness / calmness / sleepiness
2. **specks:** small particles / drops / pockets
3. **craned:** stiff / stretched / bent
4. **conjectured:** understood / asked / guessed
5. **exploit:** easy way / quiet method / risky act
6. **darted:** hid quietly / moved quickly / escaped rapidly
7. **slight:** very thin / quite small / quite deep
8. **heartily:** emotionally / sadly / with energy

Idiomatic expressions

The story uses a few interesting expressions. For instance, Holmes talks about how the student 'yielded to temptation', indicating that the person did something that he knew was wrong—in this case, he decided to copy the question paper.

A couple of other expressions that are used in the text

drawn himself erect: stood up straight

my sin had found me out: meaning that his wrongdoing had been discovered

Can you think of situations where you could use these phrases to talk about someone or something?

READING IDEAS

If you liked this story, you could read:

1. THE ADVENTURES OF SHERLOCK HOLMES by Sir Arthur Conan Doyle
2. THE HERCULE POIROT and MISS MARPLE SERIES by Agatha Christie
3. THE PERRY MASON SERIES by Erle Stanley Gardner

14
SILVER

Slowly, silently, now the moon
Walks the night in her silver **shoon**;
This way, and that, she peers, and sees
Silver fruit upon silver trees;
One by one the **casements** catch
Her beams beneath the silvery **thatch**;
Couched in his kennel, like a log,
With paws of silver sleeps the dog;
From their shadowy **cote** the white breasts peep
Of doves in a silver-feathered sleep;
A harvest mouse goes **scampering** by,
With silver claws and a silver eye;
And moveless fish in the water gleam,
By silver reeds in a silver stream.

WALTER DE LA MARE (1873–1956) was an English poet, short-story writer and a novelist.

WORDS TO KNOW

shoon: shoes

casements: windows that open on hinges

thatch: roof made of dried straw

cote: shed or shelter

scampering: moving in quick, short steps

FOR DISCUSSION

1. Why do you think everything in the poem is silver? Are all these silver things silver in daylight as well?
2. What is the mood or the feeling in the poem? Is it one of rest and peace or is it something else?

LANGUAGE

Personification

The poem uses personification—talking about a thing or animal as if it were a person.

Find some of words or lines in the poem that talk about the moon as a person, as a human being.

Rhyme scheme

The poem has a simple rhyme scheme—pairs of rhyming lines. These are called 'rhyming couplets'.

Find the rhyme scheme. As a creative exercise, try to add another line to the poem. Make sure they are a rhyming couplet.

Alliteration

The poem also uses alliteration, where a consonant sound is repeated to create a rhythm. For example, in the line 'Slowly, silently, now the moon', the repeated s sound creates a rhythm.

Can you find other examples of repeated consonants in the poem?

A silent and peaceful mood is created in the poem. The most repeated word is, of course, 'silver'; but the consonant 's' is repeated throughout the poem. This alliterative repetition of the 's' sound is called sibilance. This creates an effect of softness.

Try reading the whole poem out loud and see what effect it creates.

15
THE GRAND TRUNK ROAD

'Now let us walk,' muttered the lama, and to the click of his rosary they walked in silence mile upon mile. The lama as usual, was deep in meditation, but Kim's bright eyes were open wide. This broad, smiling river of life, he considered, was a vast improvement on the cramped and crowded Lahore streets. There were new people and new sights at every stride—people he knew and people that were altogether out of his experience.

They met a troop of long-haired, strong-scented Sansis with baskets of lizards on their backs, their lean dogs sniffing at their heels. These people kept their own side of the road, moving at a quick, furtive jog-trot. Behind them, walking wide and stiffly across the strong shadows, the memory of his leg-irons still on him, strode one newly released from the jail; his full stomach and shiny skin to prove that the Government

RUDYARD KIPLING (1865–1936) was a British poet, short-story writer and novelist. His most famous works are *Kim* and *The Jungle Book.*

This descriptive passage is taken from Rudyard Kipling's Kim, *which describes the adventures of an orphan boy Kim who travels through India with his guru, an old Tibetan Lama (priest) who is looking for a holy place in India. The story was written in 1901, more than 120 years ago. This description talks about what they see while travelling down the Grand Trunk Road. As they walk, Kim observes everything around him.*

fed its prisoners better than most honest men could feed themselves. Kim knew that walk well. Then an Akali, a Sikh devotee in the blue-checked clothes of his faith, with polished-steel **quoits** glistening on the cone of his tall blue turban, stalked past, returning from a visit to one of the independent Sikh States, where he had been singing the ancient glories of the Khalsa to College-trained princes in top-boots and white-cord breeches.

Here and there they met or were overtaken by the gaily dressed crowds of whole villages turning out to some local fair; the women, with their babes on their hips, walking behind the men, the older boys prancing on sticks of sugar-cane, dragging rough brass models of locomotives such as they sell for a halfpenny, or flashing the sun into the eyes of their betters from cheap toy mirrors. One could see at a glance what each had bought; and if there were any doubt you needed only to watch the wives comparing, brown arm against brown arm, the newly purchased dull glass bracelets that come from the North-West. These merry-makers stepped slowly, calling one to the other and stopping to haggle with sweetmeat-sellers, or to make a prayer before one of the wayside shrines—sometimes Hindu, sometimes **Mussalman***—which both creeds share with beautiful impartiality.

A solid line of blue, rising and falling like the back of a caterpillar in haste, would swing up through the quivering dust and trot past to a chorus of quick cackling. That was a gang of changars—the women who have taken all the embankments of all the Northern railways under their charge—a flat-footed, strong-limbed, blue-petticoated clan of earth-carriers, hurrying north on news of a job, and wasting no time by the road. They walked with squared elbows, swinging hips, and heads on high, as suits women who carry heavy weights.

---

* This is the term used in the original.

A little later a marriage procession would strike into the Grand Trunk with music and shoutings, and a smell of marigold and jasmine stronger even than the reek of the dust. One could see the bride's litter, a blur of red and tinsel, staggering through the haze, while the bridegroom's bewreathed pony turned aside to snatch a mouthful from a passing fodder-cart. Then Kim would join the Kentish-fire of good wishes and bad jokes, wishing the couple good fortune.

Still more interesting and more to be shouted over it was when a strolling juggler with some half-trained monkeys, or a panting, feeble bear, or a woman who tied goats' horns to her feet, and with these danced on a slack-rope, set the horses to shying and the women to shrill, long-drawn quavers of amazement.

The lama never raised his eyes. He did not note the money-lender on his goose-rumped pony, hastening along to collect the cruel interest; or the long-shouting, deep-voiced little mob—still in military formation—of soldiers on leave, rejoicing to be rid of their breeches and puttees, and saying the most outrageous things to the most respectable people in sight. Even the seller of Ganges-water he did not see, and Kim expected that he would at least buy a bottle of that precious stuff. He looked steadily at the ground, and strode as steadily hour after hour, his soul busied elsewhere.

But Kim was in the seventh heaven of joy. The Grand Trunk at this point was built on an embankment to guard against winter floods from the foothills, so that one walked, as it were, a little above the country, along a stately corridor, seeing all India spread out to left and right. It was beautiful to behold the many-yoked grain and cotton wagons crawling over the country roads: one could hear their axles, complaining a mile away, coming nearer, till with shouts and yells and bad words they climbed up the steep incline and plunged on to the hard main road, carter reviling carter.

It was equally beautiful to watch the people, little clumps of red and blue and pink and white and saffron, turning aside to go to their own villages, dispersing and growing small by twos and threes across the level plain. Kim felt these things, though he could not give tongue to his feelings, and so contented himself with buying peeled sugar-cane and spitting the pith generously about his path.

The crowd thickened as they neared the resting-place which marked the end of their day's journey. A line of stalls selling very simple food and tobacco, a stack of firewood, a police-station, a well, a horse-trough, a few trees, and, under them, some trampled ground dotted with the black ashes of old fires, are all that mark a parao on the Grand Trunk.

By this time the sun was driving broad golden spokes through the lower branches of the mango-trees; the parakeets and doves were coming home in their hundreds; the chattering, grey-backed Seven Sisters, talking over the day's adventures, walked back and forth in twos and threes almost under the feet of the travellers; and shufflings and scufflings in the branches showed that the bats were ready to go out on the night-picket. Swiftly the light gathered itself together, painted for an instant the faces and the cartwheels and the bullocks' horns as red as blood.

Then the night fell, changing the touch of the air, drawing a low, even haze, like a gossamer veil of blue, across the face of the country, and bringing out, keen and distinct, the smell of wood-smoke and cattle and the good scent of wheaten cakes cooked on ashes. The evening patrol hurried out of the police station with important coughings and **reiterated** orders; and a live charcoal ball in the cup of a wayside carter's hookah glowed red while Kim's eye mechanically watched the last flicker of the sun.

WORDS TO KNOW

quoits: rings of iron

Mussalman: Muslim

reiterated: repeated

FOR DISCUSSION

1. Do you think that such a sight as described here could be seen in India even today?

2. Why do you think the lama does not notice anyone or anything on the road? What is he busy with?
3. Why do you think Kim is fascinated by the people he sees on the road? Would you have been fascinated by these sights if you had been Kim?
4. A parao is a resting place for travellers travelling on foot by a road. What in the story tells you that the parao is a safe place for travellers, or that the safety of travellers is taken care of?
5. Think about the sights and sounds you have seen while travelling and compare them with the sights and sounds in this story.

LANGUAGE

Words and idiomatic expressions

What do the following words and phrases in the story mean?

1. **Kentish-fire of good wishes:** shouted good wishes / whispered good wishes / said good wishes
2. **embankment:** sloping road / rough and uneven surface / raised area of land
3. **to be in the seventh heaven of joy:** to be extremely happy / to be happy after a long time / to be happy for someone else
4. **to be shouted over:** to be happy about / to be amazed at / to be uninterested in
5. **give tongue to:** eat very quickly / be rude to someone / speak politely

Imagery

The author uses very powerful visual imagery to describe not just the people but also the atmosphere and the places on the road.

Read and organize the imagery used in the chapter into three groups: people, places and animals.

Personification

The author uses personification—speaking of objects or animals as if they are people—to create a powerful description.

Can you identify the following from the story?

1. birds/animals being personified
2. the sun/sunlight being personified

Similes and metaphors

The story uses this simile to describe a group of people walking in a line: A solid line of blue, rising and falling **like the back of a caterpillar in haste** ...

Can you find other similes and metaphors in the story that add depth to the description?

READING IDEAS

If you liked this story, you could read:

1. THE JUNGLE BOOK by Rudyard Kipling
2. HOWARDS END by E.M. Forster

16

THE SOLITARY REAPER

Behold her, single in the field,
Yon solitary Highland Lass!
Reaping and singing by herself;
Stop here, or gently pass!
Alone she cuts and binds the grain,
And sings a melancholy strain;
O listen! for the **Vale profound**
Is overflowing with the sound.

No Nightingale did ever chant
More welcome notes to weary bands
Of travellers in some shady haunt,
Among Arabian sands:
A voice so thrilling ne'er was heard
In spring-time from the Cuckoo-bird,
Breaking the silence of the seas
Among the farthest **Hebrides**.

Will no one tell me what she sings?
Perhaps the **plaintive numbers** flow
For old, unhappy, far-off things,
And battles long ago:
Or is it some more humble **lay**,
Familiar matter of to-day?
Some natural sorrow, loss, or pain,
That has been, and may be again?

Whate'er the theme, the Maiden sang
As if her song could have no ending;
I saw her singing at her work,
And o'er the sickle bending;
I listened, motionless and still;
And, as I mounted up the hill,
The music in my heart I bore,
Long after it was heard no more.

WILLIAM WORDSWORTH (1770–1850) was an English poet who wrote poems mostly on nature.

WORDS TO KNOW

Behold her: Look at her

Yon solitary Highland Lass: there is a lonely young girl in the mountains

Vale profound: deep valley

Hebrides: islands near Scotland

plaintive numbers: songs full of sorrow

lay: a narrative song

FOR DISCUSSION

1. The poet cannot understand what the reaper is singing, but quite likes it. Do you think you can like or appreciate a song in a language you do not understand? Why?
2. Why do you think the poet calls the song he hears, melancholy (sad) if he cannot understand the words?
3. Why do you think the reaper is singing even though she is all alone?
4. The poet compares the voice of the reaper to that of a nightingale and a cuckoo. Which bird would you compare a good singer to?
5. What do you think the last two lines mean?

LANGUAGE

Comparison

The poet uses two comparisons to talk about the song that he hears—the sounds of a nightingale and a cuckoo. These are not simple comparisons, but long and descriptive.

Can you think of another descriptive comparison that you would use to compare a singer with anything else? (HINT: Think of a natural sound that is pleasant.)

Synonyms

Instead of repeating the word 'song', the poet uses synonyms for it—strain, number, lay. Why do you think he does this?

Rhyme scheme

The general rhyme scheme in the poem for each stanza is ABABCCDD—the first four lines rhyme alternately, the fifth and sixth line rhyme with each other, as do the last two lines.

This rhyme scheme is not followed in two stanzas. Can you identify them?

17

THE OPEN WINDOW

'My aunt will be down presently, Mr. Nuttel,' said a very **self-possessed** young lady of fifteen. 'In the meantime you must try and put up with me.'

Framton Nuttel **endeavoured** to say the correct something which should flatter the niece of the moment without unduly discounting the aunt that was to come. Privately he doubted more than ever whether these formal visits on a succession of total strangers would do much towards helping the nerve cure which he was supposed to be undergoing.

'I know how it will be,' his sister had said when he was preparing to migrate to this village. 'You will bury yourself down there and not speak to a living soul, and your nerves will be worse than ever from moping. I shall just give you letters of introduction to all the people I know

H.H. Munro (Saki) (1870–1916) was a master of the short story. His stories were funny and sometimes full of mystery. He was better known by his pen name Saki.

Framton Nuttel, a visitor to the Sappleton home, has been advised to move to a quieter place by his doctor. When he talks to Mrs Sappleton's niece, what does he think?

there. Some of them, as far as I can remember, were quite nice.'

Framton wondered whether Mrs Sappleton, the lady to whom he was presenting one of the letters of introduction came into the 'nice' category.

'Do you know many of the people round here?' asked the niece, when she judged that they had had sufficient silent **communion**.

'Hardly a soul,' said Framton. 'My sister was staying here with friends some four years ago, and she told me to come and meet some of the people here.'

He made the last statement in a tone of distinct regret.

'Then you know practically nothing about my aunt?' asked the self-possessed young lady.

'Only her name and address,' admitted Mr Nuttel. He was wondering whether Mrs Sappleton was married or widowed. An undefinable something about the room seemed to suggest that a man lived here too.

'Her great tragedy happened just three years ago,' said the child. 'That would be since your sister's time.'

'Her tragedy?' asked Framton. Somehow in this peaceful spot tragedies seemed out of place.

'You may wonder why we keep that window wide open on an October afternoon,' said the niece, indicating a large **French window** that opened on to a lawn.

'It is quite warm for the time of the year,' said Framton, 'but has that window got anything to do with the tragedy?'

'Out through that window, exactly three years ago, her husband and her two young brothers went off for their day's duck hunting. They never came back. In crossing the **moor** to their favourite duck-shooting ground all three were drowned in a treacherous piece of **bog**. Their bodies were never recovered. That was the dreadful part of it.'

Here the child's voice lost its confident tone and became falteringly human. 'Poor aunt always thinks that they will come back someday, they and the little brown spaniel that was drowned with them, and walk in at that window just as they used to do. That is why the window is kept open every evening till it is

quite dusk. Poor dear aunt, she has often told me how they went out, her husband with his white waterproof coat over his arm, and Ronnie, her youngest brother, singing "Bertie, why do you bound" as he always did to tease her, because she said it got on her nerves. Do you know, sometimes on still, quiet evenings like this, I almost get a creepy feeling that they will all walk in through that window—'

She broke off with a little shudder. It was a relief to Framton when the aunt bustled into the room with a whirl of apologies for being late in making her appearance.

'I hope Vera has been amusing you?' she said.

'She has been very interesting,' said Framton.

'I hope you don't mind the open window,' said Mrs. Sappleton briskly. 'My husband and brothers will be home directly from shooting, and they always come in this way. They've been out for **snipe** in the marshes today, so they'll make a fine mess over my poor carpets.'

She rattled on cheerfully about the shooting and the scarcity of ducks, and the chances of finding them in the winter. To Framton it was all purely horrible. He made a desperate but only partially successful effort to turn the talk to a less ghastly topic. He was conscious that his hostess was giving him only a fragment of her attention, and her eyes were constantly straying past him to the open window and the lawn beyond. It was certainly an unfortunate coincidence that he should have paid his visit on this tragic anniversary.

'The doctors agree in ordering me complete rest, an absence of mental excitement, and avoidance of anything in the nature of violent physical exercise,' announced Framton, who laboured under the tolerably **widespread**

delusion that total strangers and chance acquaintances are hungry for the least detail of one's ailments and infirmities, their cause and cure. 'On the matter of diet, they are not so much in agreement,' he continued.

'No?' said Mrs. Sappleton, in a voice which only replaced a yawn at the last moment. Then she suddenly brightened into alert attention—but not to what Framton was saying.

'Here they are at last!' she cried. 'Just in time for tea, and don't they look as if they were muddy up to the eyes!'

Framton shivered slightly and turned towards the niece with a look intended to convey sympathetic comprehension. The child was staring out through the open window with a dazed horror in her eyes. In a chill shock of nameless fear Framton swung round in his seat and looked in the same direction.

In the deepening twilight three figures were walking across the lawn towards the window, they all carried guns under their arms, and one of them was additionally burdened with a white coat hung over his shoulders. A tired brown spaniel kept close at their heels. Noiselessly they neared the house, and then a hoarse young voice chanted out of the dusk: 'I said, Bertie, why do you bound?'

Framton grabbed wildly at his stick and hat. The hall door, the gravel drive, and the front gate were dimly noted stages in his headlong retreat. A cyclist coming along the road had to run into the hedge to avoid **imminent collision.**

'Here we are, my dear,' said the bearer of the white mackintosh, coming in through the window, 'fairly muddy, but most of it's dry. Who was that who bolted out as we came up?'

'A most extraordinary man, a Mr Nuttel,' said Mrs. Sappleton. 'Could only talk about his illnesses and dashed off without a word of goodbye or apology when you arrived. One would think he had seen a ghost.'

'I expect it was the spaniel,' said the niece calmly. 'He told me he had a horror of dogs. He was once hunted into a cemetery somewhere on the banks of the Ganges by a pack of pariah dogs and had to spend the night in a newly dug grave with the creatures snarling and grinning and foaming just above him. Enough to make anyone lose their nerve.'

Romance at short notice was her speciality.

WORDS TO KNOW

endeavoured: tried

French window: double window as big as a door which opens to a terrace or leads outside the house.

moor: large, open, treeless area

bog: soft, wet earth which can trap and drown people and animals

snipe: bird with a long beak

widespread delusion: false belief held by most people

imminent collision: an accident likely to happen very soon

Romance at short notice: ability to make up exciting stories quickly

FOR DISCUSSION

1. Is Mrs Sappleton's niece Vera a good storyteller?
2. Why do you think Vera decides to frighten Mr Nuttel?
3. How do you think Vera knew exactly what was going to happen?
4. If you were Mr Nuttel, what would you do after leaving the house?
5. What does the final line of this story tell you about Vera? (HINT: The word 'romance' here means 'an exciting story'.)

LANGUAGE

Read the text and circle the best meaning of these words and phrases.

1. **self-possessed:** selfish / quiet / confident / clever
2. **communion:** silence / communication / visit / politeness
3. **falteringly:** in an unsure manner / in a sad manner / in a fast manner / in a loud way
4. **bustled in:** entered slowly / entered silently / entered with confidence / entered in a hurry

Idiomatic expressions

Read this line from the story.

Framton, [...] laboured under the tolerably widespread delusion that total strangers and chance acquaintances are hungry for the least detail of one's ailments and infirmities, their cause and cure.

The author uses the **idiomatic expression** 'laboured under the delusion', to tell us that what Framton believed so strongly is actually not true. So, it is not true that 'total strangers and chance acquaintances are hungry for the least detail of one's ailments and infirmities, their cause and cure', but Framton believes it to be true.

Can you think of something which you know is not true, but many people believe strongly? Begin with 'Many people labour under the delusion that' and describe this untrue belief.

Adjectives

'Do you know many of the people round here?' asked the niece, when she judged that they had had **sufficient silent** communion.

The words **sufficient** and **silent** are adjectives used to describe the noun communion.

This story has a great number of adjectives in it. Writers use adjectives to describe things or people, to make it easy for readers to imagine the scene.

Make a list of all the adjectives that you can find in the story. Use as many of them as you can to describe a day in your life. Remember that you can describe people or things using these adjectives.

READING IDEAS

If you liked this story, you could read:

1. THE COMPLETE SHORT STORIES OF SAKI
2. COLLECTED STORIES OF O. HENRY

18

THE WAY THROUGH THE WOODS

They shut the road through the woods
Seventy years ago.
Weather and rain have undone it again,
And now you would never know
There was once a road through the woods
Before they planted the trees.
It is underneath the **coppice** and **heath**,
And the thin **anemones**.
Only the keeper sees
That, where the ring-dove broods,
And the badgers roll at ease,
There was once a road through the woods.

Yet, if you enter the woods
Of a summer evening late,
When the night-air cools on the trout-ringed pools
Where the otter whistles his mate.

(They fear not men in the woods,
Because they see so few)
You will hear the beat of a horse's feet,
And the swish of a skirt in the dew,
Steadily cantering through
The misty solitudes,
As though they perfectly knew
The old lost road through the woods ...
But there is no road through the woods.

RUDYARD KIPLING (1865–1936) was a British poet, short story writer and novelist. His most famous poems are *If* and *Gunga Din.*

READING IDEAS

coppice: trees growing close together in a group

heath (hee-th): land covered by grass and a type of plant called heather (rhymes with 'weather').

anemones (ani-moneys): plants with red and white flowers

FOR DISCUSSION

1. On reading the first stanza, what kind of feeling do you get?
2. How do you feel when you read the second stanza? Does it make you feel scared or uncomfortable?
3. The poet says that you may be able to hear the sound of horses riding through the woods at night even though there is no road through the woods. In your opinion, are the horses (and maybe riders) real?

LANGUAGE

Visual images

One of the ways the poem creates a feeling of strangeness is by using strong visual images. The first stanza has natural images of birds, plants and animals.

Which images in the second stanza create a ghostly or strange feeling in your mind?

Rhyme scheme

The poet uses an unusual rhyme scheme in the poem, which is followed in both stanzas.

Can you find one difference between the first and second stanza which changes the rhyme scheme? (There may be unfamiliar words at the end of the lines. Use a dictionary to check their pronunciation.)

Rhythm

One of the interesting things that gives a rhythm to the poem is internal rhyme. This is when a word in the middle of a line rhymes with a word at the end of the same line. One example from the poem is 'Weather and rain have undone it again'.

Can you find more such examples of internal rhyme in the poem?

19

THE PIECE OF STRING

In Goderville it was market-day. In the public square of Goderville there was a crowd of human beings and animals mixed together. The horns of the cattle, the tall hats of the peasants and the headgear of the peasant women rose above the surface of the assembly. And the clamorous, shrill, screaming voices made a continuous and savage din.

Master Hauchecome of Breaute had just arrived at Goderville, and he was walking towards the public square when he **perceived** upon the ground a little piece of string. Master Hauchecome, was economical, and thought that everything useful ought to be picked up. He bent painfully, for he suffered from rheumatism. He took the bit of thin cord from the ground and began to roll it carefully when he noticed Master

GUY DE MAUPASSANT (1850-1893) was a French short-story writer. He is known for the incisive understanding of human nature he brought to his short stories.

Set in a small village, this story is about a period in the life of an old peasant. What happens when he sees a piece of string on the ground and picks it up?

Malandain, the harness maker, on the threshold of his door, looking at him. They were on bad terms, both being good haters.

Master Hauchecome was seized with a sort of shame to be seen thus by his enemy, picking a bit of string out of the dirt. He concealed his 'find' quickly under his shirt, then in his trousers' pocket. Then he pretended to be still looking on the ground for something which he did not find, and he went toward the market, his head forward, bent double by his pains.

He was soon lost in the noisy and slowly moving crowd which was busy with interminable bargainings. Soon, little by little, the square was deserted, and when the bell rang at noon, those who had stayed too long scattered to their shops.

At Jourdain's the great room was full of people eating, as the big court was full of vehicles of all kinds, carts, gigs, wagons, dumpcarts, yellow with dirt, mended and patched, raising their shafts to the sky like two arms or perhaps with their shafts in the ground and their backs in the air.

Just opposite the diners seated at the table, the immense fireplace, filled with bright flames, cast a lively heat on the backs of the row on the right. The appetizing odour of food increased the joviality and made everybody's mouth water. Everyone ate there at Master Jourdain's. The dishes were passed and emptied. Everyone talked about their affairs, their purchases and sales. They discussed the crops.

Suddenly the drum beat in the court before the house. After the public crier had ceased his drumbeating he called out: 'It is hereby made known to the inhabitants of Goderville, and in general to all persons present at the market, that there was lost this morning on the road to Benzeville, between nine and ten o'clock, a black leather pocketbook containing five hundred francs and some business papers. The finder is requested to return same with all haste to the mayor's office or to Master Fortune Houlbreque of Manneville. There will be twenty francs reward.'

Then the man went away. The heavy roll of the drum and the crier's voice were again heard at a distance. Then they began to discuss the chances that Master Houlbreque had of finding his pocketbook. They were finishing their coffee when a chief of the **gendarmes** arrived.

He inquired: 'Is Master Hauchecome of Breaute here?'

Master Hauchecome, seated at the other end of the table, replied: 'Here I am.'

And the officer resumed: 'Master Hauchecome, will you have the goodness to accompany me to the mayor's office? The mayor would like to talk to you.'

The peasant, surprised and disturbed, rose and, even more bent than in the morning, for the first steps after each rest were specially difficult, set out, repeating: 'Here I am, here I am.'

The mayor was awaiting him, seated on an armchair. 'Master Hauchecome,' said he, 'you were seen this morning to pick up, on the road to Benzeville, the pocketbook lost by Master Houlbreque of Manneville.'

The countryman, astounded, looked at the mayor, already terrified by this suspicion resting on him without his knowing why.

'Me? Me? Me pick up the pocketbook?'

'Yes, you yourself.'

'Word of honour, I never heard of it.'

'But you were seen.'

'I was seen, me? Who says he saw me?'

'Master Malandain, the harness maker.'

The old man remembered, understood and flushed with anger.

'Ah, he saw me pick up this string here, Sir.' And rummaging in his pocket, he drew out the little piece of string.

But the mayor, incredulous, shook his head.

'You will not make me believe, Master Hauchecome, that Master Malandain, who is a man worthy of credence, mistook this cord for a pocketbook.'

The peasant, furious, lifted his hand, repeating: 'It is nevertheless the truth of the good God, the sacred truth, Sir.'

The mayor resumed: 'After picking up the object you stood looking a long while in the mud to see if any piece of money had fallen out.'

The good old man choked with indignation and fear.

'How can anyone tell—how can anyone tell—such lies to take away an honest man's reputation! How can anyone—'

There was no use in his protesting. Nobody believed him. At his own request Master Hauchecome was searched. Nothing was found on him.

Finally, the mayor, discharged him with the warning that he would consult the public prosecutor and ask for further orders.

The news had spread. As he left the mayor's office the old man was surrounded and questioned with a serious or **bantering** curiosity. He began to tell the story of the string. No one believed him. They laughed at him.

They said: 'Old rascal, get out!'

And he grew angry, becoming exasperated, hot and distressed at not being believed, not knowing what to do and repeating himself.

He started on his way back with three neighbours to whom he pointed out the place where he had picked up the bit of string, and all along the road, he spoke of his adventure.

In the evening he took a walk around the village of Breaute in order to tell it to everybody. He only met with **incredulity**. It made him ill at night.

The next day about one o'clock in the afternoon, a hired man in the employ of Master Breton returned the pocketbook and its contents to Master Houlbreque of Manneville. This man claimed to have found the object in the road, but not knowing how to read, he had carried it to the house and given it to his employer.

The news spread through the neighbourhood. Master Hauchecome was informed of it. He immediately went around and began to recount his story completed by the happy climax. He was in triumph.

'What grieved me so much was not the thing itself as the lying. There is nothing so shameful as to be placed under a cloud on account of a lie.'

He talked of his adventure all day long; he told it on the highway to people who were passing by, and to persons coming out of church the following Sunday. He stopped strangers to tell them about it. He was calm now, and yet something disturbed him. People did not seem convinced. He seemed to feel that remarks were being made behind his back.

On Tuesday of the next week he went to the market at Goderville, urged solely by the necessity he felt of discussing the case. Master Hauchecome told his tale to a farmer who did not let him finish and said to his face: 'You big rascal.'

Master Hauchecome was confused. Why was he being called a big rascal?

When he was seated at the table in Jourdain's tavern he **commenced** to explain 'the affair'.

A horse dealer called to him: 'That's an old trick. I know all about your piece of string!'

Hauchecome stammered: 'But the pocketbook was found.'

But the other man replied: 'Shut up. There is one that finds and there is one that reports. At any rate you are mixed with it.'

The peasant suddenly understood. They accused him of having had the pocketbook returned by a confederate, by an **accomplice**.

He tried to protest. All the table began to laugh. He could not finish his dinner and went home ashamed and indignant, choking with anger and confusion. His innocence seemed impossible to prove.

Each day he retold his adventure, prolonging his history every day, adding each time new reasons, more energetic protestations, more solemn oaths which he imagined and prepared in his hours of solitude, his whole mind given up to the story of the string. He was believed so much the less as his defence was more complicated and his arguing more subtle.

He felt it, consumed his heart over it and wore himself out with useless efforts. He wasted away before their very eyes. The **wags** now made him tell about the string to amuse them, as they make a soldier who has been on a campaign tell about his battles. His mind, affected to the depth, began to weaken. Towards the end of December he took to his bed.

He died in the first days of January, and in the delirium of death he kept claiming his innocence, reiterating:

'A piece of string, a piece of string—look—here it is, Sir.'

WORDS TO KNOW

perceived: seen
gendarmes: French word for police
bantering: friendly and humorous
incredulity: disbelief
commenced: started
accomplice: a person who helps another to commit a crime
wags: people who gossip

FOR DISCUSSION

1. Why was Master Hauchecome embarrassed about being seen picking up the string?
2. Why do you think no one believed Master Hauchecome?
3. Do you think people would have forgotten the matter if Master Hauchecome had stopped talking about it?
4. What does the story tell you about the way rumour operates?
5. If you had known about the piece of string, would you have believed Master Hauchecome?
6. Was it just bad luck that Master Hauchecome was held to be guilty?
7. What would you do if you were ever unjustly accused of doing something wrong?

LANGUAGE

Choose the correct meaning of these words and phrases from the story.

1. **clamorous:** colourful / noisy / crowded
2. **interminable:** quick / serious / unending
3. **joviality:** happy mood / seriousness / feelings of anger
4. **worthy of credence:** capable of—being trusted / being famous / being truthful
5. **rummaging:** searching in a hurry / searching with care / searching unknowingly

Idiomatic expressions

Master Hauchecome talks about how he was 'placed under a cloud' because of a lie. This is an idiomatic expression that means he was mistrusted because he was thought to have done something wrong.

Here are a few other idiomatic expressions used in the story. Can you find the meanings of these?

1. with all haste
2. flushed with anger
3. met with incredulity
4. was in triumph
5. consumed his heart
6. took to his bed
7. behind his back
8. affected to the depth

READING IDEAS

If you liked this story, you could read:

1. THE COMPLETE SHORT STORIES OF GUY DE MAUPASSANT
2. THE GREATEST SHORT STORIES OF ANTON CHEKHOV

20

THE BATTLE OF BLENHEIM

It was a summer evening,
Old Kaspar's work was done,
And he before his cottage door
Was sitting in the sun,
And by him **sported** on the green
His little grandchild Wilhelmine.

She saw her brother Peterkin
Roll something large and round,
Which he beside the rivulet
In playing there had found;
He came to ask what he had found,
That was so large, and smooth, and round.

Old Kaspar took it from the boy,
Who stood **expectant** by;
And then the old man shook his head,
And, with a natural sigh,

‘’Tis some poor fellow’s skull,’ said he,
‘Who fell in the great victory.

‘I find them in the garden,
For there’s many here about;
And often when I go to plough,
The **ploughshare** turns them out!
For many thousand men,’ said he,
‘Were slain in that great victory.’

‘Now tell us what ’twas all about,’
Young Peterkin, he cries;
And little Wilhelmine looks up
With wonder-waiting eyes;
‘Now tell us all about the war,
And what they fought each other for.’

‘It was the English,’ Kaspar cried,
‘Who put the French to rout;
But what they fought each other for,
I could not well make out;
But everybody said,’ quoth he,
‘That ’twas a famous victory.

'My father lived at Blenheim then,
Yon little stream **hard by**;
They burnt his dwelling to the ground,
And he was forced to fly;
So with his wife and child he fled,
Nor had he where to rest his head.

'With fire and sword the country round
Was wasted far and wide,
And many a **childing** mother then,
And new-born baby died;
But things like that, you know, must be
At every famous victory.

'They say it was a shocking sight
After the field was won;
For many thousand bodies here
Lay rotting in the sun;
But things like that, you know, must be
After a famous victory.
'Great praise the Duke of Marlbro' won,
And our good Prince Eugene.'
'Why, 'twas a very wicked thing!'
Said little Wilhelmine.

'Nay ... nay ... my little girl,' quoth he,
'It was a famous victory.

'And everybody praised the Duke
Who this great fight did win.'
'But what good came of it at last?'
Quoth little Peterkin.
'Why that I cannot tell,' said he,
'But 'twas a famous victory.'

ROBERT SOUTHEY (1774–1843) an English poet, is remembered for this poem and *The Story of the Three Bears*, the original version of *Goldilocks and the Three Bears.*

WORDS TO KNOW

sported: here, sat
expectant: waiting.
ploughshare: blade of a plough
hard by: nearby
childing: about to give birth

FOR DISCUSSION

1. How would you have felt if you were Peterkin or Wilhelmine who found a skull in the ground?
2. Who do you agree with in your perspective about the battle—Kaspar or his granddaughter Wilhelmine?
3. Do you think that Kaspar really thinks the battle was a great and famous victory?

LANGUAGE

Refrain

The poem constantly repeats the terms 'great victory' and 'famous victory'. This repetition of a phrase is called a 'refrain'. A refrain is used to emphasize the central theme of the poem.

In this case, the rest of the poem shows us the horrors of war. So what effect does the positive refrain have?

Rhyme scheme

The poem uses six-line stanzas with a unique rhyme scheme. Identify this rhyme scheme.

21

THE STORM

MIRANDA. If by your **art**, my dearest father, you have
Put the wild waters in this roar, allay them.
The sky, it seems, would pour down stinking pitch,
But that the sea, mounting to the welkin's cheek,
Dashes the fire out. O, I have suffered
With those that I saw suffer: a brave vessel,
Who had, no doubt, some noble creature in her,
Dash'd all to pieces. O, the cry did knock
Against my very heart. Poor souls, they perish'd.
Had I been any god of power, I would
Have sunk the sea within the earth or ere
It should the good ship so have swallow'd and
The fraughting souls within her.

art: here, magic

WILLIAM SHAKESPEARE (1564–1616) was an English poet and playwright. He is often called the Bard of Avon. Some of his famous plays are *Hamlet*, *King Lear* and *Macbeth*.

This extract is from Shakespeare's play The Tempest. *The play opens with a group of people on a ship trying to escape a tempest, but the ship splits and apparently sinks. The scene we are about to read is the second scene of the play. Prospero the magician and his daughter Miranda are standing on the island near which the tempest is raging.*

PROSPERO. **Be collected:**
No more amazement: tell your piteous heart
There's no harm done.

MIRANDA. O, woe the day!

PROSPERO. No harm.
I have done nothing but in care of thee,
Of thee, my dear one, thee, my daughter, who
Art ignorant of what thou art, nought knowing
Of **whence** I am, nor that I am more better
Than Prospero, master of a full poor **cell**,
And thy no greater father.

MIRANDA. More to know
Did never meddle with my thoughts.

PROSPERO. 'Tis time
I should inform thee farther. Lend thy hand,
And pluck my magic garment from me.—So:
[*Lays down his mantle*]
Lie there, my **art**. Wipe thou thine eyes; have comfort.
The **direful** spectacle of the wreck, which touch'd
The very virtue of compassion in thee,
I have with such provision in mine art
So safely ordered that there is no soul—
No, not so much **perdition** as an hair
Betid to any creature in the vessel

Be collected: remain calm

Art: here, old form of 'are'

whence: old form of 'from where'

cell: here, a small hut

mantle: a sleeveless cloth worn over other clothes

art: here, heart

direful: terrible, horrible

perdition: disaster or hurt

Betid: happened

Which thou heard'st cry, which thou saw'st sink. Sit down;
For thou must now know farther.

MIRANDA. You have often
Begun to tell me what I am, but stopp'd
And left me to a **bootless inquisition**,
Concluding 'Stay: not yet.'

PROSPERO. The hour's now come;
The very minute bids thee **ope** thine ear;
Obey and be attentive. Canst thou remember
A time before we came unto this cell?
I do not think thou canst, for then thou wast not
Out three years old.

MIRANDA. Certainly, sir, I can.

PROSPERO. By what? by any other house or person?
Of any thing the image tell me that
Hath kept with thy remembrance.

MIRANDA. 'Tis far off
And rather like a dream than an assurance
That my remembrance warrants. Had I not
Four or five women once that tended me?

PROSPERO. Thou hadst, and more, Miranda. But how is it
That this lives in thy mind? What seest thou else
In the dark backward and **abysm** of time?
If thou remember'st ought **ere** thou camest here,
How thou camest here thou mayst.

MIRANDA. But that I do not.

> **bootless inquisition:** useless inquiry
>
> **ope**: open
>
> **abysm:** dark, deep hole
>
> **ere:** before

PROSPERO. Twelve year since, Miranda,
twelve year since,
Thy father was the Duke of Milan and
A prince of power.

MIRANDA. O the heavens!
What foul play had we, that we came from
thence?
Or blessed was't we did?

PROSPERO. Both, both, my girl:
By foul play, as thou say'st, were we heaved
thence,
But blessedly **holp** hither.

MIRANDA. O, my heart bleeds
To think o' the teen that I have turn'd
you to,
Which is from my remembrance! Please you,
farther.

PROSPERO. My brother and thy uncle, call'd Antonio—
I pray thee, mark me—that a brother should
Be so **perfidious!**—he whom next thyself
Of all the world I loved and to him put
The manage of my state; as at that time
Through all the **signories** it was the first
And Prospero the prime duke, being so reputed
In dignity, and for the liberal arts
Without a parallel; those being all my study,
The government I cast upon my brother

holp: helped

perfidious: treacherous, deceitful

signories: areas ruled by a lord

And to my state grew stranger, being transported
And rapt in secret studies. Thy false uncle—
Dost thou attend me?

MIRANDA. Sir, most heedfully.

PROSPERO. Being once perfected how to grant suits,
How to deny them, who to advance and who
To trash for over-topping, new created
The creatures that were mine, I say, or changed 'em,
Or else new form'd 'em; having both the key
Of officer and office, set all hearts i' the state
To what tune pleased his ear; that now he was
The ivy which had hid my princely trunk,
And suck'd my verdure out on't. Thou attend'st not.

MIRANDA. O, good sir, I do.

PROSPERO. I pray thee, mark me.
I, thus neglecting worldly ends, all dedicated
To closeness and the bettering of my mind
With that which, but by being so retired,
O'er-prized all popular rate, in my false brother
Awaked an evil nature; and my trust,
Like a good parent, did beget of him
A falsehood in its contrary as great
As my trust was; which had indeed no limit,
A confidence sans bound. He being thus lorded,
Not only with what my revenue yielded,
But what my power might else exact, like one
Who having into truth, by telling of it,

Prospero and Miranda are put into a rotten boat without any way of rowing it, and then left to die.

Made such a sinner of his memory,
To credit his own lie, he did believe
He was indeed the duke; out o' the substitution
And executing the outward face of royalty,
With all prerogative: hence his ambition growing—
Dost thou hear?

MIRANDA. Your tale, sir, would cure deafness.

PROSPERO. To have no screen between this part he play'd
And him he play'd it for, he needs will be
Absolute Milan. Me, poor man, my library
Was dukedom large enough: of temporal royalties
He thinks me now incapable; confederates—
So dry he was for sway, wi' the King of Naples
To give him annual tribute, do him homage,
Subject his coronet to his crown and bend
The dukedom yet unbow'd—alas, poor Milan!—
To most ignoble stooping.

MIRANDA. O the heavens!

PROSPERO. Now the condition.
The King of Naples, being an enemy
To me inveterate, hearkens my brother's suit;
Which was, that he, in lieu o' the premises
Of homage and I know not how much tribute,
Should presently extirpate me and mine
Out of the dukedom and confer fair Milan
With all the honours on my brother: whereon,
A treacherous army levied, one midnight

Prospero explains how his brother became powerful and influential, by figuring out who to punish and who to encourage. Eventually Prospero's brother became so powerful that everyone listened to him.

Fated to the purpose did Antonio open
The gates of Milan, and, i' the dead of darkness,
The ministers for the purpose hurried thence
Me and thy crying self.

MIRANDA. Alack, for pity!
I, not remembering how I cried out then,
Will cry it o'er again: it is a hint
That wrings mine eyes to't.

PROSPERO. Hear a little further
And then I'll bring thee to the present business
Which now's upon 's; without the which this story
Were most impertinent.

MIRANDA. Wherefore did they not
That hour destroy us?

PROSPERO. Well demanded, wench:
My tale provokes that question. Dear, they durst not,
So dear the love my people bore me, nor set
A mark so bloody on the business, but
With colours fairer painted their foul ends.
In few, they hurried us aboard a bark,
Bore us some leagues to sea; where they prepared
A rotten carcass of a boat, not rigg'd,
Nor tackle, sail, nor mast; the very rats
Instinctively have quit it: there they hoist us,
To cry to the sea that roar'd to us, to sigh
To the winds whose pity, sighing back again,
Did us but loving wrong.

MIRANDA. Alack, what trouble
Was I then to you!

PROSPERO. O, a **cherubim**
Thou wast that did preserve me. Thou didst smile.
Infused with a **fortitude** from heaven,
When I have deck'd the sea with drops full salt,
Under my burthen groan'd; which raised in me
An undergoing stomach, to bear up
Against what should ensue.

cherubim: angel
fortitude: courage

MIRANDA. How came we ashore?

PROSPERO. By Providence divine.
Some food we had and some fresh water that
A noble Neapolitan, Gonzalo,
Out of his charity, who being then appointed
Master of this design, did give us, with
Rich garments, linens, stuffs and necessaries,
Which since have steaded much; so, of his gentleness,
Knowing I loved my books, he furnish'd me
From mine own library with volumes that
I prize above my dukedom.

MIRANDA. Would I might
But ever see that man!

PROSPERO. Now I arise:
[*Resumes his mantle*]
Sit still, and hear the last of our sea-sorrow.
Here in this island we arrived; and here

Have I, thy schoolmaster, made thee more profit
Than other princesses can that have more time
For vainer hours and tutors not so careful.

MIRANDA. Heavens thank you for't! And now, I pray you, sir,
For still 'tis beating in my mind, your reason
For raising this sea-storm?

PROSPERO. Know thus far forth.
By accident most strange, bountiful Fortune,
Now my dear lady, hath mine enemies
Brought to this shore; and by my **prescience**
I find my zenith doth depend upon
A most auspicious star, whose influence
If now I court not but omit, my fortunes
Will ever after droop. Here cease more questions:
Thou art inclined to sleep; 'tis a good dulness,
And give it way: I know thou canst not choose.
[*Miranda sleeps*]

prescience: ability to see the future

FOR DISCUSSION

1. Before the storm, Prospero has not told his daughter the details of how they arrived at the island. Why do you think this was?
2. Why do you think Miranda remembers being taken care of by two or three women, and nothing else?
3. Do you think that Prospero was right to pay all his attention to learning and magic?

4. Now that the people who betrayed Prospero are within his power, what do you think will happen?
5. How do you think Miranda would feel now that she knows her own history? How would you feel?

LANGUAGE

Dramatic ideas

As Prospero speaks, he keeps asking Miranda if she is listening. Why is he doing that? (HINT: Think about the fact that these are lines to be spoken by the same actor in a play. What would happen if Miranda does not speak at all in between?)

Iambic pentameter

If you read the play aloud, you will see that each line follows the same rhythm—in fact, almost the same number of syllables occur in each line. So, though there is no rhyme, there is a fixed rhythmic pattern to the lines. Let's take a look at some lines.

If by your art, my dearest father, you have
Put the wild waters in this roar, allay them. ...
Thou hadst, and more, Miranda. But how is it
That this lives in thy mind? What seest thou else
In the dark backward and abysm of time?

If you count the syllables in each line here, and through the play, you will realize that each line generally has ten or eleven syllables. This type of verse is called 'iambic pentameter'.

Read the play to find how the pattern lends a flow and rhythm to the dialogue.

Images

Shakespeare uses a large number of images in his play. Even in this short scene, we can find a few. Let's look at the first one.

The sky, it seems, would pour down stinking pitch,
But that the sea, mounting to the welkin's cheek,
Dashes the fire out.

Here the image created is of a dark sky which is pitch black and lighted by flashes of lightning, put out by the water in the sky. This image also contains a personification—the welkin (sky) is said to have a cheek.

Can you find more such images in the excerpt?

READING IDEAS

If you liked this excerpt, you could read:

1. TALES FROM SHAKESPEARE by Charles and Mary Lamb OR THE COMPLETE WORKS OF SHAKESPEARE
2. SAINT JOAN by Bernard Shaw
3. FIVE PLAYS FOR CHILDREN by Vijay Tendulkar

Answers

Page 15
1. against the rules of 2. to decide 3. in a serious way 4. think and believe strongly

Page 22
1. wet and muddy 2. angry 3. loud enough to be heard 4. in a serious manner 5. serious

Page 32
1. burnt 2. tied up 3. extremely poor 4. in an angry way 5. quickly 6. eating 7. replied 8. sadly 9. going away quietly

Page 42
1. marked 2. the money had been stolen 3. pirates 4. rudeness 5. ambitious 6. shouted 7. start an attack

Page 47
1. like 2. laughed loudly

Page 59
1. a soft knock 2. dark space 3. spending 4. lazy 5. funny 6. attractive sight 7. completely interested 8. lying down 9. not reduced 10. having a bad effect on

Page 65
1. make happy 2. shameful 3. entertain 4. a stupid plan 5. shocking 6. the most terrible part 7. huge 8. riches

Page 77
1. restlessness 2. small particles 3. stretched 4. guessed 5. risky act 6. escaped rapidly 7. quite small 8. with energy

Page 87
1. shouted good wishes 2. raised area of land 3. to be extremely happy 4. to be amazed at 5. be rude to someone

Page 99
1. confident 2. communication 3. in an unsure manner 4. entered in a hurry

Page 111
1. noisy 2. unending 3. happy mood 4. capable of being trusted 5. searching in a hurry

IMAGE CREDITS

CHRISTINA ROSSETTI: Dante Gabriel Rossetti, Public domain, via Wikimedia Commons

CHARLES KINGSLEY: Charles Watkins _Wellcome_V0026646, CC BY 4.0 via Wikimedia Commons

LEWIS CARROLL: Oscar Gustave Rejlander, Public domain

ROBERT LOUIS STEVENSON: Henry Walter Barnett, Public domain

CHARLES DICKENS: Rischgitz, Public domain, via Wikimedia Commons

EMILY DICKINSON: Unknown author, Public domain, via Wikimedia Commons

JEROME K. JEROME: National Media Museum from UK, No restrictions, via Wikimedia Commons

EDWARD LEAR: Edward Lear, Public domain, via Wikimedia Commons

LOUISA MAY ALCOTT: George Kendall Warren; restored by Adam Cuerden, Public domain, via Wikimedia Commons

JONATHAN SWIFT: Charles Jervas, Public domain, via Wikimedia Commons

EDGAR ALBERT GUEST: NBC Radio, Public domain, via Wikimedia Commons

ARTHUR CONAN DOYLE: Elliott & Fry, Public domain, via Wikimedia Commons

WALTER DE LA MARE: Lady Ottoline Morrell (died 1938), Public domain, via Wikimedia Commons

RUDYARD KIPLING: Elliott & Fry, Public domain, via Wikimedia Commons

WILLIAM WORDSWORTH: William Shuter, Public domain, via Wikimedia Commons

H.H. MUNRO (SAKI): Nicholas95, CC BY-SA 3.0, via Wikimedia Commons

GUY DE MAUPASSANT: Nadar, Public domain, via Wikimedia Commons

ROBERT SOUTHEY: Edward Nash, Public domain, via Wikimedia Commons

WILLIAM SHAKESPEARE: Martin Droeshout, Public domain, via Wikimedia Commons

List the books you've read from the ones excerpted here.

List your favourite passages from the books excerpted here.

List any other classics you've read and your favourite one.

Can you match the authors of some popular English classics with their works?

A.

1. The Pickwick Papers, A Christmas Carol

B.

2. I'm Nobody! Who Are You?, A Bird, Came Down the Walk

C.

3. The Necklace, Two Friends

D.

4. The Hound of the Baskervilles, The Poison Belt

E.

5. Through the Looking-Glass, Jabberwocky

[ANSWERS: A – 5; B – 1; C – 4; D – 2; E – 3]

ALSO BY RUSKIN BOND

"Wherever I go, I meet young writers, or young people who want to write, and they are always asking questions. Someone who has survived as a writer for seventy years must have something to offer by way of "tips" (as one young friend put it) or the lessons learnt from all the ups and downs of a literary journey."

How To Be A Writer is peppered with nuggets of practical advice for every person who is aspiring to write and be published – all told in Ruskin Bond's characteristic understated, tongue-in-cheek, humorous style.

So, what is it that a person requires the most to become a writer? A love of books, of language, of life, an observant eye and a good memory along with enthusiasm, optimism and persistence.

How To Be A Writer is an exclusive glimpse into the writing credo of Ruskin Bond, an author who has had an incredibly successful writing career spanning over 70 years.

30 Years *of*

HarperCollins*Publishers*India

At HarperCollins, we believe in telling the best stories and finding the widest possible readership for our books in every format possible. We started publishing 30 years ago; a great deal has changed since then, but what has remained constant is the passion with which our authors write their books, the love with which readers receive them, and the sheer joy and excitement that we as publishers feel in being a part of the publishing process.

Over the years, we've had the pleasure of publishing some of the finest writing from the subcontinent and around the world, and some of the biggest bestsellers in India's publishing history. Our books and authors have won a phenomenal range of awards, and we ourselves have been named Publisher of the Year the greatest number of times. But nothing has meant more to us than the fact that millions of people have read the books we published, and somewhere, a book of ours might have made a difference.

As we step into our fourth decade, we go back to that one word – a word which has been a driving force for us all these years.

Read.

Harper Collins · 4th · HARPER PERENNIAL · HARPER BUSINESS · HARPER BLACK · हार्पर हिन्दी

HarperCollins *Children'sBooks* · HARPER DESIGN · HARPER VANTAGE · Harper Sport